THE DEVELOPMENT OF SOCIAL NETWORK ANALYSIS

A STUDY IN THE SOCIOLOGY OF SCIENCE

Linton C. Freeman

ΣP

Empirical Press
Vancouver, BC Canada

Library of Congress Control Number: 2004111710
Publisher: BookSurge, LLC
North Charleston, South Carolina
ISBN 1-59457-714-5

ΣP Empirical Press, Vancouver, BC Canada
Cover and book design by Rosemary Boyd, Document Design
        Laguna Beach, CA

"We all connect, like a net we cannot see."

—Mickenberg and Dugan,
Taxi Driver Wisdom, 1995

Jacob L. Moreno

Harrison C. White

This work is dedicated to Jacob L. Moreno and Harrison White. Without the mammoth contributions of these two scholar-teachers there would be no field of social network analysis.

Contents

Figures

Preface

This book was produced with a great deal of help from a lot of people. Many of the early practitioners of the social network approach allowed themselves to be interviewed—either face-to-face, or by telephone, email or regular old-fashioned letter mail. These include Peter Abell, John Barnes, Russ Bernard, Peter Blau, Liz Bott, John Boyd, Kathleen Carley, Doc Cartwright, Jim Davis, Alain Degenne, Pat Doreian, Tom Fararo, Claude Flament, Michel Forsé, Ove Frank, Sue Freeman, Bill Garrison, Torsten Hägerstrand, Maureen Hallinan, Muriel Hammer, Frank Harary, Paul Holland, Charles Kadushin, Larry Kincaid, Al Klovdahl, Ed Laumann, Hal Leavitt, Sam Leinhardt, Joel Levine, Nan Lin, Larissa Lomnitz, Duncan Luce, Bob Merton, Clyde Mitchell, Rob Mokken, Woody Pitts, Charles Proctor, Anatol Rapoport, Ev Rogers, Arnold Simel, Tom Snijders, Frans Stokman, Morry Sunshine, Chuck Tilley, Barry Wellman, Doug White, Harrison White, Al Wolfe and Rolf Ziegler. A good many of these people went to great pains to produce detailed accounts of who influenced them to think in the structural perspective of social network analysis. These individuals provided most of the information that has gone into the present historical account.

In addition, I received useful feedback from a number of people after I presented a preliminary version of this historical review at the International Sunbelt Social Network Conference in Vancouver, BC, on April 12, 2000. The detailed written suggestions provided by Davor Jedlicka, Peter Marsden, Frans Stokman and Barry Wellman were particularly helpful. And a good many colleagues have read all or parts of this manuscript and provided useful feedback. These include John Barnes, Mike Brower, Katie Faust, Sue Freeman, Irving Louis Horowitz, Dominic Jesse, Charles Kadushin, Bob Merton, Cal Morrill, Woody Pitts, Ev Rogers, M. de Lourdes Sosa, Cindy Webster, Doug White, Robin Williams and, most of all, Morry Sunshine, who has worked harder than anyone could reasonably expect.

Beyond this relatively recent input, I learned a great deal from earlier discussions I had with others who were involved in the development of social network analysis but who are no longer available to be interviewed. Among these, my conversations with Gregory Bateson, Jim Coleman, St. Clair Drake, Fred Kochen, Paul Lazarsfeld, Jiri Nehnevajsa, Ithiel de Sola Pool, Tom Schweizer and Bill Whyte are particularly memorable. Each had an impact on my thinking about the field.

I am also grateful to Rosemary Boyd who designed and edited this book. Without her wise counsel this would be a far less polished essay.

In an important way, all of these individuals are co-authors of this book. All provided key information and insights. With all this help, then, I hope that the present account is mostly accurate. Any inaccuracies that remain are my own.

Linton C. Freeman, Laguna Beach, CA
Holmes Beach, FL

Chapter 1

Introduction

Writing in 1968, a Columbia University sociologist, Allen Barton, described mainstream research in social science:

> *For the last thirty years, empirical social research has been dominated by the sample survey. But as usually practiced, using random sampling of individuals, the survey is a sociological meatgrinder, tearing the individual from his social context and guaranteeing that nobody in the study interacts with anyone else in it. It is a little like a biologist putting his experimental animals through a hamburger machine and looking at every hundredth cell through a microscope; anatomy and physiology get lost, structure and function disappear, and one is left with cell biology....If our aim is to understand people's behavior rather than simply to record it, we want to know about primary groups, neighborhoods, organizations, social circles, and communities; about interaction, communication, role expectations, and social control.*

Barton's statement was true when he made it, and it is still true today. Mainstream social research was and is focused exclusively on the behavior of individuals. It neglects the *social* part of behavior; the part that is concerned with the ways individuals interact and the influence they have on one another.

Fortunately for those of us who don't want to grind up the social world into hamburger, there is, and there has always been, an alternative. Some social research has consistently focused on the social relationships linking individuals rather than on the individuals themselves. The kind of research that examines the links among the objects of study is called *structural*.

This kind of structural approach is not confined to the study of human social relationships. It is present in almost every field of science. Astrophysicists, for example, study the gravitational attraction of each planet in the solar system on each of the others in order to account for planetary orbits. Molecular chemists examine how various kinds of atoms interact together to form different kinds of molecules. Electrical engineers observe how the interactions of various electronic components—like capacitors and resistors—influence the flow of current through a circuit. And biologists study the ways in which each of the species in an ecosystem interacts with and impinges on each of the others.[1]

In social science, the structural approach that is based on the study of interaction among social actors is called social network analysis. The relationships that social network analysts study are usually those that link individual human beings. But important social relationships may link social individuals that are not human, like ants or bees or deer or giraffes or apes. Or they may link actors that are not individuals at all. Network analysts often examine links among groups or organizations—even among nation-states or international alliances.

The social network approach is grounded in the intuitive notion that the patterning of social ties in which actors are embedded has important consequences for those actors. Network analysts, then, seek to uncover various kinds of patterns. And they try to determine the conditions under which those patterns arise and to discover their consequences.

The idea that the patterning of social ties is worth examining is probably very old. For example, descent lists are stressed

---

[1] As early as 1925, for example, the philosopher-mathematician Alfred North Whitehead (1925, p. 297) suggested that, "A forest is the triumph of the organisation of mutually dependent species."

both in the Bible and in the education of Hawaiian nobles, who were required to memorize dozens of generations of their forebears.

Before modern social network analysis emerged, investigators used one or some combination of four approaches in conducting structural research on social phenomena. Some clarified and extended the basic structural intuition. Some collected the kind of actor-by-actor data that permits the systematic examination of social patterning. Some developed procedures for constructing visual images of patterns of ties. And others worked on computation or spelled out the mathematical properties of social patterns.

But it is only recently that these approaches have all been integrated into an organized paradigm for research. All four of these features are found in modern social network analysis, and together they define the field:

1. Social network analysis is motivated by a structural intuition based on ties linking social actors,

2. It is grounded in systematic empirical data,

3. It draws heavily on graphic imagery, and

4. It relies on the use of mathematical and/or computational models.

Beyond commitment to these four features, however, modern social network analysts also recognize that a wide range of empirical phenomena can be explored in terms of their structural patterning. But coming to that recognition has been a difficult process. In an interview in 1996, the anthropologist Clyde Mitchell described his own experience when he personally came to see the generality and broad utility of the network analytic approach. In the 1950s he had been a participant in Max Gluckman's seminar at the University of Manchester. There, several of the participants had used a structural approach to guide their research. But, at that point, Mitchell failed to see the generality of that approach; he viewed those research reports as interesting but he failed to see their underlying identity.

Then, a few years later, in the early 1960s, Mitchell was directing the research of several ethnographic fieldworkers in Zimbabwe (Mitchell, 1969). They included David Boswell, Peter Harries-Jones, Bruce Kapferer and Pru Wheeldon. Boswell was collecting data on personal crisis and social support. Harries-Jones was concerned with the importance of tribalism in political organization. Kapferer was studying a labor conflict in a mining company. And Wheeldon was examining the emergence of political processes in an inter-ethnic community. On the face of it, these were simply four unrelated research projects.

But at that point, Mitchell had a breakthrough. He began to see that, as structural studies, all four projects shared a common core. As he put it:

> ...it was then that I realized that we needed a formal method of conducting the analyses. I had been reading the journal Sociometry, so I knew something about those procedures, but of course I knew very little. And it was then that Doc Cartwright and Frank Harary's book (Harary, Norman and Cartwright, 1965) appeared that I learned to get on to it.

Once the social network research community began to recognize the generality of its structural approach, useful applications in a very wide range of empirical situations became possible. As I indicated in a recent piece in the *Encyclopedia of Psychology* (Freeman, 2000a), the network field has developed important applications in research on:

> ...the study of occupational mobility, the impact of urbanization on individuals, the world political and economic system, community decision-making, social support, community, group problem-solving, diffusion, corporate interlocking, belief systems, social cognition, markets, sociology of science, exchange and power, consensus and social influence, and coalition formation...primate studies, computer-mediated communication, intra- and inter-organizational studies, and marketing...health and illness, particularly AIDS.

The ever-widening range of applications of social network analysis is demonstrated in a study by Otte and Rousseau (2002). They examined network analytic articles published between 1984 and 1999. Figure 1.1 shows that, year-by-year, there has been an almost linear growth in the number of substantive areas in which the social network approach has been applied.

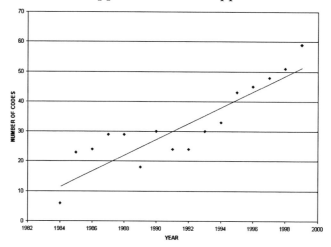

Figure 1.1. Association between number of substantive areas specified and year of publication of social network research

In effect, then, social network analysis is defined not only by the four features listed above, but also by an extremely wide and ever-growing range of applications. Its practitioners increasingly share recognition of the broad generality of its structural paradigm.

Because of this generality, network analysis cuts across the boundaries of traditional disciplines. It brings together sociologists, anthropologists, mathematicians, economists, political scientists, psychologists, communication scientists, statisticians, ethologists, epidemiologists, computer scientists, both organizational behavior and market specialists from business schools and recently, physicists. These people come from vastly different backgrounds but they all share a common commitment to the structural perspective embodied in the network approach.

This shared commitment is demonstrated by the systematic accumulation of knowledge within the field. Social network analysis is one of the few social science endeavors in which people influence one another in such a way that they all work together to build a cumulative body of knowledge. Indeed, after examining its citation practices, Hummon and Carley (1993) went so far as to declare network analysis a "normal" science in the sense described by Thomas Kuhn (1962). Kuhn defined a science as normal if and only if it displays a systematic approach that both generates puzzles and solves them. Since a normal science is the product of an ordered sequence of discoveries, it is cumulative.

Social network analysts now have an international organization, the *International Network for Social Network Analysis*, or *INSNA*.[2] *INSNA* holds an annual meeting in Europe or in North America and it is involved in the publication of three professional journals, *Social Networks, Connections* and the electronic *Journal of Social Structure*. Beginning in the early 1980s with books by Steven D. Berkowitz (1982) and David Knoke and James H. Kuklinski (1982), writers began to produce standard texts on social network analysis. Texts now have been written in several languages including English, French, German, Italian, Finnish and Swedish. An up-to-date list is available on an INSNA web page:

http://www.sfu.ca/~insna/INSNA/books_inf.html

There are also a large number of computer programs designed specifically for the analysis and display of social networks. See the INSNA web page:

http://www.sfu.ca/~insna/INSNA/soft_inf.html

---

[2]A Spanish-language affiliate of INSNA, REDES, was formed in the late 1990s. It organizes meetings and publishes a social network journal. REDES also has a web page: http://www.redes-sociales.net/

In addition, a number of centers for network training and research have sprung up throughout the world. They are listed on an INSNA web page:

http://www.sfu.ca/~insna/INSNA/schools_inf.html

All of this growth leaves us with some interesting questions. Beyond the very old intuitive idea of the importance of social ties, where did this interest and activity begin? What are the intellectual foundations of the field? How and when were various kinds of structural studies brought together into a coherent program of research? And how did that research get organized into a recognized collective enterprise that includes organizations, meetings, books and journals and the like?

So far, no one has produced a comprehensive history of the origins, development and emergence of this field. There are a few brief historical notes in print, but each of them tends to focus on only a part of the whole picture. Some (Leinhardt, 1977; Berkowitz, 1982; Marsden and Lin, 1982; Freeman, 1989; Scott, 1992; Degenne and Forsé, 1994; Wasserman and Faust, 1994) were concerned with the question of the origins of social network analysis. These writers have sought to uncover how and when the key ideas and procedures of the field were developed. Others (Mullins and Mullins, 1973; Wolfe, 1978; Alba, 1982; Marsden and Lin, 1982) were primarily interested in questions of institution building. They tried to figure out how and when the intellectual ideas were organized into an established field of research.

Some of the writers who have examined the question of the origins of social network analysis have proposed that it all began in the early 1930s with the work of Jacob Moreno (Hummon and Carley, 1993; Leinhardt, 1977; Marsden and Lin, 1982; Freeman, 1989; Degenne and Forsé, 1994; Wasserman and Faust, 1994). The year in question is 1934 when Moreno's introduction to sociometry, *Who Shall Survive?*, was published. Clearly, that publication was a signal event in the history of social network analysis. It was a turning point for the development of the field.

But other writers have argued that social network analysis did not begin until the early 1970s when Harrison White began training graduate students at Harvard (Mullins and Mullins, 1973; Berkowitz, 1982; Scott, 1992). During that era, White, along with his students, produced an amazing number of important contributions to social network theory and research. Contemporary network analysis could never have emerged without those contributions.

Both of these events do turn out to have produced points of critical transition in the history of the field. Both involved contributions that provided turning points for the development of social network research. I treat these two periods of critical transition in great detail. But there is much more, as well. In this book I also highlight a great deal of important work that took place before the 1930s, and crucial developments that occurred between the 1940s and 1960s. Many of these are fascinating examples of the development of science, and they also underline the importance of social ties and social gaps in the development of a scientific specialty.

In this book I will examine contributions in four distinct eras: (1) the period ending in the late 1920s, (2) the 1930s, (3) the period from 1940 to the end of the 1960s, and (4) the period from the early 1970s to the present.

Chapter 2 will examine the contributions of the people who worked before the 1930s. These are the people who introduced key ideas and practices that anticipated current social network research.

Chapters 3 and 4 will review the birth of modern social network analysis. Two, probably independent, developments all started in the late 1920s and ran through the 1930s. One of these, examined in Chapter 3, was the introduction of sociometry by Jacob L. Moreno and his associates. A second, outlined in Chapter 4, took place at Harvard and was led by W. Lloyd Warner.

Chapters 5, 6 and 7 will cover the 1940s, 1950s and 1960s respectively. In those chapters, I will review social network research that took place during the "dark ages" between the contributions of the 1930s and those of the 1970s. And then Chapter 8 will return to Harvard and examine the transformations that Harrison White and his students produced in the early 1970s.

Chapter 9 will take up the question of institution building. I will examine what happened to the field after the 1970s. There the issue is how the network approach became a recognized field of research. Finally, Chapter 10 will attempt to bring it all together and reexamine some of the surprising results that were revealed in the earlier chapters.

As a final note, I need to stress that this book is not intended as an intellectual history of social network analysis. It is, rather, an exploration of the field from a sociology of science perspective. I am convinced that the patterning of links among the people who were involved in the development of the field—its social network—is a key to understanding how and why it emerged. So I have tried to reconstruct those patterns. Of course, I could not avoid dealing with a good many elements of intellectual history, but my primary aim here is to uncover the social processes that were involved in the emergence of a scientific specialty. Thus, this is a history of social network analysis written from a social network perspective.

Chapter 2

Prehistory: The Origins of Social Network Ideas and Practices

In the first chapter I defined social network analysis as an approach to social research that displays four features: a structural intuition, systematic relational data, graphic images and mathematical or computational models. In this chapter I will consider each of those four features in turn and try to specify its first use in social research. My aim here is to describe the earliest research I have been able to find that embodied each feature.

Much of the research described here will include work that is often cited—work done by people who are usually credited with having paved the way for social network analysis. Other research I will describe, however, was produced by people who are relatively unknown in the network field, people who are not usually recognized as having introduced an idea or practice, but who did innovate in ways that provide precursors of current network research practices. These are people whose contributions have not been—but perhaps should be—acknowledged.

2.1 Early Structural Intuitions

In a previous report (Freeman, 1989, p. 18), I reproduced a descent list from the Book of Genesis. My aim there was to suggest that human beings have, since the earliest days, recognized the importance of the ties that link social actors. But that early recognition was implicit.

The earliest explicit statement of a structural perspective on social life that I have found was proposed by Isidore Auguste Marie François Xavier Comte (usually known simply as Auguste Comte). Comte is pictured in Figure 2.1. Although he is usually not mentioned in reviews of the history of social network analysis, I suspect that he had a large, albeit indirect, influence on the development of the field.

Comte was born in 1798 in Montpellier in the south of France. He was the eldest son in a middle class family. He entered the *lycée*—the equivalent of high school—at the age of nine, and studied mathematics with Daniel Encontre. Comte was always an outstanding student, but from his earliest days in school he also established himself as a something of a rebel.

Despite his rebellious tendencies, Comte scored fourth among 300 applicants and was admitted to France's top technical college, the *Ecole Polytechnique*, when he was sixteen (Boiteux, 1958). There he continued to study mathematics and he continued to excel. But this was a period of political unrest in France and as a result, the whole *ecole* was closed two years later in 1816. For a year Comte supported himself by tutoring. Then in 1817, at the age of nineteen, he met and went to work with Henri Saint-Simon.

Figure 2.1. Auguste Comte honored on a French postage stamp

Saint-Simon was then sixty years old. He was an established utopian thinker and is generally acknowledged as the founder of French socialism. According to Coser (1977, p. 15), Saint-Simon was "creative" and "fertile," but at the same time was a "disorderly and tumultuous man." Comte brought order and discipline into the partnership and the two worked and published together for seven years. During most of that period Comte lived in the VIth arrondissement in Paris. His

Figure 2.2. Plaque at Comte's Paris residence[3]

regard in France is demonstrated by the fact that his residence is still memorialized with the marble plaque shown in Figure 2.2.

Coser (pp. 1–17) described the collaboration between Saint-Simon and Comte:

> A number of scholars have argued the question of who benefited the most from the close collaboration, Comte or Saint-Simon. There is no need to take sides in this somewhat byzantine quarrel. It suffices to say that Comte was influenced in a major way by his patron, even though his close contact with Saint-Simon may have brought to fruition ideas that had already germinated in Comte's mind....The sketches and essays that Comte wrote during the years of close association with Saint-Simon, especially between 1819 and 1824, contain the nucleus of all his later major ideas.

---

[3]In English, this plaque reads, "Auguste Comte, founder of positivism, lived here from 1818 until 1822. Here he conceived the sociological law of three states and formulated the system of classification of the sciences."

Comte's primary commitment was to the development of sociology as a science. In that respect his views are quite contemporary, although they were published first between 1830 and 1842 (Comte, 1830–42).[4] Comte coined the term *sociology* and he specified its goal as uncovering the laws of society. This goal, he argued, required both theory and systematic observation. On the importance of theory he said (Martineau, 1853/2000, v. II, p. 203) "No real observation of any kind of phenomena is possible, except in as far as it is first directed, and finally interpreted, by some theory." And about observation, he indicated that the study of social phenomena (Martineau, 1853/2000, v. II, p. 181) "...supposes first, that we have abandoned the region of metaphysical idealities, to assume the ground of observed realities by a systematic subordination of imagination to observation."

Comte argued also for the importance of systematic comparative research in sociology. He (Martineau, 1853/2000, v. II, p. 207) went so far as to suggest comparing the social structures of human beings with those of non-human animals, "It is a very irrational disdain which makes us object to all comparison between human society and the social state of the lower animals." This view is consistent with some of the latest work in social network analysis (Faust and Skvoretz, 2002).

In his definition of sociology, Comte specified the two main aspects of the field, *statics* and *dynamics*. Statics, he said (Martineau, 1853/2000, v. II, pp. 192, 204 and 207), is focused on the investigation of the "laws of social interconnection" or (v. II, p. 183) "the laws of action and reaction of the different parts of the social system." At the most fundamental level, according to Comte, these parts are nuclear families. He argued (Martineau, 1853/2000, v. II, p. 234) that since

> *...every system must be composed of elements of the same nature with itself, the scientific spirit forbids us to regard society as composed of individuals. The true*

---

[4]In the present work I have drawn heavily on a new edition of the translation of Comte's *Cours de philosophie positive* by Harriet Martineau (1853/2000). Comte liked Martineau's translation of his work so much that he substituted Martineau's two-volume version for his own six-volume version in his list of books that he believed should survive forever (Standley, 1981, p. 160).

> *social limit is certainly the family—reduced, if neces-*
> *sary, to the elementary couple which forms its basis.*

Comte (Martineau, 1853/2000, v. II, p. 187) went on to show
how the parts of the social system are interconnected: "Families
become tribes and tribes become nations." His view, then, is strik-
ingly contemporary. He defined society using the kinds of structural terms that are found today in social network analysis.
Whether he is given credit or not, Comte was the first scholar I
could find that proposed a way of looking at society in terms of
the interconnections among social actors.

Most other prominent nineteenth and early twentieth century sociologists embraced Comte's structural perspective. A
common theme involved describing differences in the patterning of social connections in traditional versus modern societies.
In his study of ancient law, for example, Sir Henry Maine (1861/
1931) did just that. He suggested that in small traditional, fami-
ly-oriented societies, individual ties were governed by univer-
sal rights and obligations; these arrangements he called *status*.
In contrast, he saw most ties in large modern societies as grounded on negotiated agreements; in his terms, they are based on
contract.

Ferdinand Tönnies (1855/1936) made a similar distinction
when he used the word *gemeinschaft* to characterize the traditional social form that involved personal and direct social ties
that linked individuals who shared values and beliefs. He contrasted that with modern forms based on *gesellschaft*, where social links are formal, impersonal and instrumental.

Emile Durkheim (1893/1964) described traditional societies in which *solidarité mechanique* linked similar individuals with
repressive regulations. This he distinguished from modern societies in which a division of labor led individuals to form coop-
erative links based on *solidarité organique*.

Sir Herbert Spencer (1897) in England and Charles Horton
Cooley (1909/1962) in America both described traditional small-
scale societies in which individuals were linked by intimate, *primary* relations. And they both contrasted those with modern,
large-scale societies where individuals are often linked by impersonal, *secondary* relations.

These early sociologists all tried to specify the different kinds of social ties that link individuals in different forms of social collectivities. Thus, since they were all concerned with social linkages, they all shared a structural perspective.

An entirely different structural perspective was developed at about the same time by Gustave LeBon (1897/1995). LeBon examined the phenomenon of crowd behavior. He suggested that when individuals become members of crowds they lose their individual identities. As members of crowds, people imitate those around them, he said, and ideas and behaviors diffuse from person to person by a process of contagion. Thus, since LeBon focused on the flow of information among individuals, his concern was also structural.

Perhaps the most explicitly structural perspective adopted by any of the late nineteenth and early twentieth century social thinkers was displayed in the work of Georg Simmel (pictured in Figure 2.3). Simmel (1908/1971, p. 23) said, "Society exists where a number of individuals enter into interaction." He (pp. 24–25) went on to specify this idea:

Figure 2.3. Georg Simmel

> *A collection of human beings does not become a society because each of them has an objectively determined or subjectively impelling life-content. It becomes a society only when the vitality of these contents attains a form of reciprocal influence; only when one individual has an effect, immediate or mediate upon another, is mere spatial aggregation or temporal succession transformed into society. If, therefore, there is to be a science whose subject matter is society and nothing else, it must exclusively investigate these interactions, these kinds and forms of sociation.*

In these statements Simmel expressed the core belief that underlies modern social network analysis. For Simmel, sociology was no more and no less than the study of the patterning of interaction. And Simmel's student, Leopold von Wiese (Wiese and Mueller, 1931/1941, p. 30), went even further and talked in contemporary terms about a "system of relations" and a "network of lines between men." The views expressed by Simmel and his students, then, were—and remain—explicit statements of the social network perspective.

Overall, then, there were a good many early writers— particularly in the field of sociology—who laid out the intuitive groundwork for network analysis. Early contributions, however, were not limited to intuitive ideas. In the next section I will show some early work that involved the systematic collection of structural data.

2.2 Systematic Empirical Data

At the beginning of the nineteenth century, long before Comte defined a structural approach to sociology, systematic data on social structure were being collected by a Swiss naturalist, Pierre Huber. Huber was born in Geneva, Switzerland, in 1777. His father, François Huber, was an entomologist who was deeply involved in the study of honeybees. The elder Huber became blind in 1773 at the age of twenty-three. Nevertheless, he continued his research by drawing on the observational skills of his wife, Marie Lullin, and his servant, François Burnens. With their help as observers, Huber published a major work based on systematic observation of honeybees (Huber and Bonnet, 1792). That publication had enough impact that he was thereafter known as "Huber des abeilles (Huber of the bees)." Even now his contributions are honored with a walkway named "François Huber" off the rue de Saint-Victor in Geneva.[5]

Young Pierre was raised in this household—one that was almost totally focused on the systematic observation of insect behavior. It is no wonder then that he went on to a distinguished career in entomology. At twenty-four, he published a detailed

---

[5]There is even a recently published historical novel, *The Beekeeper's Pupil* by Sara George (2003), about the life of François Huber.

description of bumblebees (1802). He observed and reported every aspect of their anatomy and life cycle in painstaking detail. And included in that description was a thorough report of their dominance behavior with respect to one another. This, so far as I have been able to discover, provides the earliest example of a report of patterned social interaction based on systematic observation.

Pierre Huber went on to work with ants (1810) and achieved world fame as a naturalist. In fact, Charles Darwin (1859, Chapter VIII) described him "as a better observer even than his celebrated father." The younger Huber's work set the stage for the development of the ethological approach in biology. At the same time, it was a precursor of two developments that have become parts of contemporary social network analysis. First, studies of social patterning among nonhuman animals continues in social science. It was picked up first by Moreno's sociometric community in the 1940s (see the special issue of *Sociometry*, Volume VIII, Number 1, February 1945). Moreover, recent research in network analysis still includes observation-based studies of the patterning of social linkages among nonhumans. And second, network analysts still conduct systematic studies of dominance. Huber's work, then, provided a model for later research in both biology and social network analysis.

The earliest example of systematic data collection on humans came a half-century later. The lawyer-anthropologist Lewis Henry Morgan was born near Aurora in upstate New York in 1818. He attended Union College where he joined a secret society called the "Grand Union of the Iroquois." Members wanted to model the form of their organization after the Iroquois, but discovered that little was known about that form.

So several members of the society, including Morgan, went to nearby Iroquois reservations to learn what they could about Iroquois social practices. And soon Morgan found himself deeply involved in the fieldwork. He ended up publishing an ethnography of the Iroquois (1851).

At that point, Morgan left off his anthropological pursuits. He moved to Rochester and began the practice of law. But the 1856 meeting of the American Association for the Advancement of Science took place in Albany, and according to Tooker (1997), that meeting revived Morgan's interest in the field. Morgan presented a paper on the Iroquois descent system at the meeting in 1858. His conclusion was that the Iroquois system of naming kin and reckoning descent was dramatically different from that used by western Europeans.

Later that year, on a trip to Michigan, Morgan interviewed an Ojibwa woman and discovered that the Ojibwa had yet another distinct scheme for naming kin and reckoning descent. For Morgan, these differences provided enough motivation to determine his future career. He began to travel in order to interview representatives of other North American tribes. At the same time, he went to great effort to enlist the help of others in collecting data in other parts of the world. When he had amassed a mammoth collection of data, he quit his law practice and devoted his time to the task of bringing all the data together. The result was a huge volume, *Systems of Consanguinity & Affinity of the Human Family* (1871/1997).

In that book Morgan reported the terms used in describing lineages of peoples throughout the world. He presented data and proposed that kinship terminologies embodied various patterns and were correlated with forms of marriage and rules of descent.

A century later, John Atkinson Hobson (1894/1954) developed an approach to uncovering links among organizations. Hobson was born in 1858 in Derbyshire, England. He earned an M.A. degree at Lincoln College, Oxford. He taught literature in Faversham and Exeter until 1887 when he moved to London. There, he joined the Fabian Society and found a job as a reporter for the Manchester Guardian newspaper.

By the time he arrived in London, Hobson had already established a reputation for his liberal views on economics. He had published books on poverty and unemployment, and he had produced a major work on capitalism—one that was often cited by Lenin (Hobson 1894/1954). As part of his treatment of capitalism, Hobson (p. 271) presented systematic data on overlapping directorships among members of "the small inner ring of South African finance." His table is reproduced as Figure 2.4.

	De Beers.	Premier.	Rand Mines.	Goldfields.	Chartered Company.
Beit, A.	I	—	I	—	I
Jameson, L. S. ...	I	—	—	—	I
Maguire, R. ...	—	—	—	I	I
Michell, Sir L. L.	I	—	—	—	I
Neumann, S. ...	—	I	I	—	—
Wernher	I	—	I	—	—

Figure 2.4. Hobson's two mode data

It shows the five major South African companies and the six board members that linked them.[6]

Thus, Hobson innovated by presenting two-mode (board member by company) data that reveal links of individuals to companies. At the same time, these data display links among the companies in terms of their shared board members as well as links among the individuals who are co-members of the same boards. Hobson, then, was the first investigator to collect systematic data on corporate interlocks. Both of these innovations are still major parts of contemporary social network analysis (Levine, 1972; Stokman, Ziegler and Scott, 1985).

The next several contributions all came from developmental and educational psychologists who worked in the 1920s. During those years, large long-term grants were made to the child-welfare institutes at the Universities of Iowa and Minnesota, Yale, Columbia Teachers College and the University of California, Berkeley (Renshaw, 1981). One result of this funding was a huge increase in the amount of research focused on children, and a good deal of that new research was centered on the study of children's interpersonal relationships.

These works are for the most part unrecognized in the field of social network research, but they did succeed in innovating a

---

[6]Fennema and Schijf (1978/79) credited Otto Jeidels (1905) with "the first extensive and systematic study on corporate interlocks." They did mention that Hobson's research was earlier, but they described it as "very partial." But since Jeidels opened his report with a quotation from Hobson, the direct line of influence is clear.

number of important network ideas and practices. In a study of homophily among school children, for example, John C. Almack (1922) developed a way of using interviews to collect network data. He asked children in a class to name those they would like to invite to a party. Then he examined the data in terms of the similarities between choosers and those chosen. Thus, Almack anticipated by more than ten years the data collection procedure usually credited to Moreno. Questions of this sort continue to provide a standard method for collecting data in network analysis. And, by examining the similarities between the choosers and the chosen, Almack anticipated the very keen interest of contemporary network analysts in homophily as a basis for social choice.

Beth Wellman[7] (1926) collected network data by recording systematic observations of who played with whom among preschool children during periods of free play. She pioneered, then, in extending Huber's ethological approach to the study of human interaction. In network analysis involving human subjects, data generated by questioning actors are common, but observational data of social links are still gathered.

Helen Bott[8] (1928) went even further, refining Beth Wellman's approach in several ways. First, she used ethnographic methods to uncover the various forms of interaction that occurred regularly among preschool children. These methods enabled her to limit systematic observations to the specific kinds of interaction relevant in the context of her research. Second, she was the first to employ a focal-child method for collecting detailed observations of who displayed each particular form of interaction with whom. Thus, she was able to avoid many of the biases inherent in other methods of observing interaction (Altmann, 1973). And third—eighteen years before Forsyth and Katz (1946) suggested using matrices to record interaction patterns—Bott recorded her data in matrix form. Although Bott apparently had little direct influence on the development of social network re-

---

[7]Beth Wellman was not a relative of Barry Wellman, who is treated in later chapters.

[8]Helen Bott was the mother of Elizabeth Bott, a major figure in social network analysis. Elizabeth was one of the experimental subjects in Helen Bott's research. Interestingly, Elizabeth Bott denies that her mother's work had any influence on her involvement with the social network perspective.

search, and is seldom if ever cited by network analysts, she certainly anticipated many modern sophisticated methods of data collection and presentation.[9]

In 1933 Elizabeth Hagman brought these two approaches to data collection—observation and interview—together. She explicitly raised a data-related issue that is still a central concern among contemporary network analysts. She observed which children played with which others during a period of free play. Then, at the end of the school term, she interviewed each child. They were asked to name who their playmates had been at the beginning of the term, in the middle of the term and at the end of the term. She then compared the observed data with the reports and examined the discrepancy between the two. that the discrepancy she found defined a research problem that remains a key issue to a great many recent investigators in the social network field (Bernard, Killworth, Kronenfeld and Sailer, 1985; Freeman, Romney and Freeman, 1987).

2.3 Graphic Imagery

Graphic images have had an important place in structural studies from the earliest days (Freeman, 2000b). The earliest examples were all focused on kinship. Christine Klapisch-Zuber (2000) showed that tree-based images were drawn as early as the ninth century. Those early images, designed to display the general patterning of kinship, showed pictorially the proximity between the occupants of any two kin categories. Klapisch-Zuber (2000, p. 37) went on to report that by the thirteenth century, drawings of trees were commonly used to depict the lineages of particular families. So the application of imagery in examining kinship began very early.

The data on kinship collected by Lewis Henry Morgan were described above. However, Morgan not only collected a huge amount of data on kinship terminology, he drew diagrams to try to specify the positions of equivalent relatives. His drawing

---

[9]Bott's contributions are recognized by developmental psychologists (Renshaw, 1971), but until her work was rediscovered by Freeman and Wellman (1995), the only citation from any social network analyst to Helen Bott that I could locate was made by Eliot D. Chapple (1940).

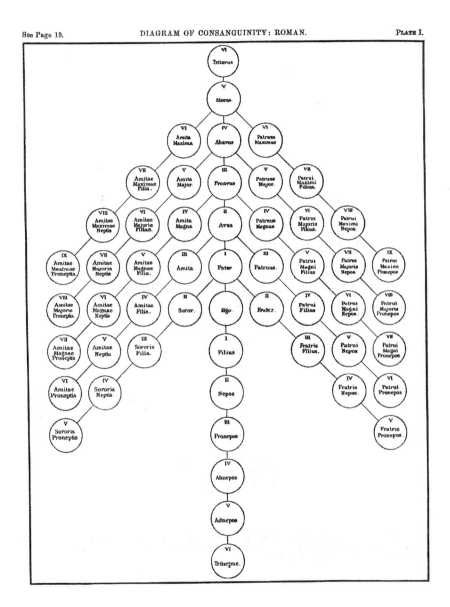

Figure 2.5. Morgan's descent system of ancient Rome

of the system of descent in ancient Rome is shown in Figure 2.5. In it, positions are drawn as circles and descent is shown by lines. Clearly, this image is an ancestor of contemporary pictures of social networks.

Near the end of the nineteenth century, Alexander Macfarlane (1883) developed a formal model of the British kinship system. Macfarlane was born in Ontario, Canada, in 1851. He received a DSc degree from the University of Edinburgh, and stayed on as a Lecturer in Mathematics there. In 1878 he became a Fellow of the Royal Society of Edinburgh, but left Scotland in 1893 to become a Professor of Physics at Texas University (now the University of Texas).

Macfarlane was an algebraist, and his work on kinship was primarily algebraic, but a part of that work involved constructing visual representations of various degrees of kinship. In the illustration shown in Figure 2.6, Macfarlane specified all the two-step marriage relationships that are prohibited in English law. From left to right, the picture shows that the law prohibits a male (designated by a +) from producing offspring with his granddaughter, his sister or his grandmother. Put another way, it prohibits a woman (○) from producing a child with her grandfather, her brother or her grandson. In the figure a short line

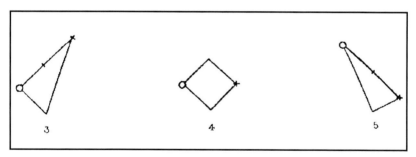

Figure 2.6. Macfarlane's images of two-step marriage prohibitions

crossing a longer one simply designates a person of either sex in another generation.

Both of these early attempts produced images of graph-like structures. They both used points to represent social actors and lines to represent linkages among them. In both cases, however, the images as they were drawn were not quite graphs. The whole meaning in a graph is in its structure—which point shares an edge with which other point. So when they are drawn, graphs place points in locations that are arbitrary; their relative positions—above, below, left or right—have no meaning. But both Morgan and Macfarlane drew images that were oriented top to bottom. Both placed genealogical antecedents higher on the page and descendants lower. Nonetheless, their images anticipated the pictures produced by network analysts using graph theory.

Hobson's (1894/1954) data on interlocking directorates was described in Section 2.2 above. But Hobson not only collected a new kind of data, he went on to introduce a way to display two-mode network data. He drew on the data shown in Figure 2.4 along with data from another table in his book and produced a picture of overlaps, a hypergraph, to show his readers how a small number of large corporations—notably the De Beers Group and Rand Mines—could use interlocking directorates to control many other firms. That hypergraph is shown in Figure 2.7. As far as I can discover, it is the earliest example of an image of

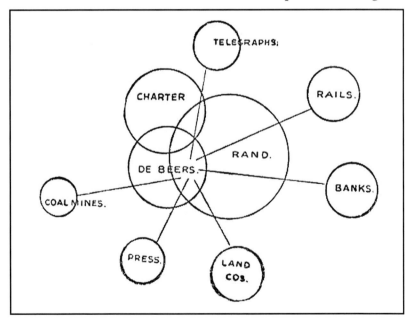

Figure 2.7. Hobson's hypergraph

overlaps used to display social patterning. Images of this sort are still widely used in social network analysis.

2.4 Mathematical and Computational Models

Unlike many other approaches to social research, network analysis has consistently drawn on various branches of mathematics both to clarify its concepts and to spell out their consequences in precise terms. The earliest application of mathematics to a problem of social structure that I have been able to uncover was algebraic.

Macfarlane was mentioned above in the discussion of early graphic tools. Those graphics, however,

Figure 2.8. Sir Francis Galton, on the right, 1909, with Karl Pearson[10]

were secondary to his main contribution. Macfarlane (1883) worked out an explicit way of characterizing the English system of kinship by concatenating kin terms. He began with a simple symbolic system:

> *There are two fundamental relationships of the highest generality, namely,* child *and* parent, *the one relationship being the reciprocal of the other. These can be combined so as to express any of the complex relationships; thus grandchild is expressed as child of child...let* c *be used to denote child,* p *to denote parent, and let "of" be expressed by juxtaposition, then grandchild will be expressed by* cc.

---

[10]Pearson (1914, 1924, 1930), the famous statistician, wrote a three-volume biography of Galton.

Macfarlane made his system more complex and more interesting by adding a notation for gender, *m* and *f*. Then he went on to designate the incest prohibitions specified under English law using his system of symbols and drawings. An example was shown in Figure 2.6.

At that time, one of the leading figures in the British scientific community was Sir Francis Galton, pictured in Figure 2.8. Galton worked as an African explorer, a meteorologist, a geographer, an anthropometrist, a statistician and a geneticist. Like many of his nineteenth century colleagues, he was something of a racist. His belief that almost all human characteristics are inherited led him to develop the controversial notion of eugenics. As a consequence, he is less respected in the current world than he might otherwise have been.

Galton was born in 1822 to a well-to-do Quaker family in Birmingham, England. He was a gifted child and, following his mother's desire, he began the study of medicine as an apprentice at the age of sixteen. He attended medical school at Kings College and Trinity College, Cambridge.

Galton transferred his medical studies to London, but when his father died in 1844, he dropped out of school and used his inheritance to become a gentleman-explorer. He explored in Southwestern Africa, and his successes promoted his recognition by the members of the scientific community. In 1856, when he was thirty-four, he was elected a Fellow of the British Royal Academy.

The most profound influence in his life occurred in 1859 when his cousin, Charles Darwin, published the *Origin of the Species*. As Galton later recalled:

> *The publication in 1859 of the* Origin of Species *by Charles Darwin made a marked epoch in my own mental development, as it did in that of human thought generally. Its effect was to demolish a multitude of dogmatic barriers by a single stroke, and to arouse a spirit of rebellion against all ancient authorities whose positive and unauthenticated statements were contradicted by modern science.*

From then on, Galton's major pursuit involved the study of inheritance, which led indirectly to his contributions to the development of tools for social network analysis. It led, for example, to a concern with kinship. So when Macfarlane presented his paper at a meeting of the Royal Anthropological Institute in 1883, Galton was present. And the minutes of the meeting show that Galton was the major discussant of Macfarlane's paper. The minutes paraphrased Galton's remarks:

> *Dr. Macfarlane had attacked the problem of relation-ship with thoroughness, ability, and success, and that he had done a very acceptable work for all who concerned themselves with genealogies of the complicated descriptions referred to by Dr. Macfarlane. The diagrammatic form seemed to himself the most distinctive and self-explanatory.*

So Galton was involved in Macfarlane's presentation, but soon thereafter he made his own contribution. He participated in developing an early probability-based model in the social network area. Galton had been working on the problem of hereditary genius, and had noticed that families that were prominent at one time seemed to decline—even disappear—at later times. He had enough mathematical training to suspect that such disappearances were the result of some probabilistic process, but he was not a good enough mathematician to spell out the process.

Consequently Galton enlisted the help of the Reverend Henry William Watson, who was both a minister and a statistician. Galton and Watson (1875) took a stochastic approach to the study of networks. Galton put the problem as follows:

> *Let $p_0, p_1, p_2, \dots$ be the respective probabilities that a man has 0, 1, 2,...sons, let each son have the same probability for sons of his own and so on. What is the probability that the male line is extinct after r generations?*

Drawing on probability theory, Watson built a stochastic model of the disappearance of family names—a network process.

His model was essentially computational; his solution involved assigning values to their basic parameters and deriving a numerical solution based on those parameters.

Watson began with the notion of a population of family names. He proposed a set of parameters involving the probabilities of a given man producing 0, 1, 2,…, q male offspring. From these properties, Watson calculated the expected proportions of each surname in each succeeding generation. Of course, any surname holder who produced no male offspring would contribute to the reduction of representatives of his name in succeeding generations. So Watson was able to show that, simply by a random process of reproduction, "We have a continual extinction of surnames going on." His conclusion was that any family name would ultimately disappear with a probability of 1.

Among network analysts, Galton and Watson are traditionally credited with having been the first to solve the problem of the disappearance of family names (Mullins and Mullins, 1973, p. 257). But, as Kendall (1974) documented, that credit is misplaced. There were two important limitations of the Galton and Watson work. First it was incomplete, and second it was actually preceded by an earlier work that had produced a more complete answer.

In 1845, a French demographer and mathematician, Irénée Jules Bienaymé, had already examined the same problem (Heyde and Seneta, 1977, p. vii). Bienaymé's work was motivated by reports by Doubleday (1842) and de Châteauneuf (1845) both of whom had observed that the surnames of noble families tend to disappear over time. Bienaymé developed a model designed to explain that observation. He said (translation by Heyde and Seneta, 1977, pp. 117–118):

> If…the mean of the number of male children who replace the number of males of the preceding generation were less than unity, it would be easily realized that families are dying out due to the disappearance of the members of which they are composed. However, the analysis shows further that when this mean is equal to unity families tend to disappear, although less rapidly…The analysis also shows clearly that if the mean

ratio is greater than unity, the probability of the extinction of families with the passing of time no longer reduces to certainty. It only approaches a finite limit, which is fairly simple to calculate and which has the singular characteristic of being given by one of the roots of the equation (in which the number of generations is made infinite) which is not relevant to the question when the mean ratio is less than unity.

This last point illustrates the incompleteness of the later Galton and Watson work. Watson dealt only with the case in which the mean number of male children was equal to one. His conclusion that names would always disappear is true only under that condition or when the number is less than one.

It is interesting to speculate about why the work of Bienaymé was lost and why Galton and Watson have traditionally been given credit for solving the problem. The answer, I think, lies in the relative prominence of Bienaymé and Galton. Bienaymé spent most of his career working as a French civil servant. He did publish mathematical papers, but relatively infrequently; there were thirty-four in all. Moreover, it was not until late in his career that he received any academic recognition at all: in 1848 he was awarded a temporary appointment as Professor of the Calculus of Probabilities at the Sorbonne, and in 1852 he was elected to the *Académie des Sciences de Paris* (Heyde and Seneta, 1977, p. 7).

In contrast, Galton came from a prominent family and was a major figure in the British Academy from the time he was in his early thirties. Moreover, he produced, "...considerably more than a hundred and seventy publications..." (Galton, 1908, Chapter XX). It is clear, then, that Galton's relative prominence put him in a much better position to be recognized and remembered. Some justice is evident, however, in the fact that in current works by probabilists the problem of the disappearance of lineages is called the "Bienaymé-Galton-Watson process."

The materials introduced in this chapter are all early examples of important innovations in each of the four features that characterize contemporary network analysis. Various early writers (1) produced structural intuitions, (2) collected systematic who-to-whom data, (3) produced graphic images of structural forms and (4) developed both mathematical and computational models.

Some, like Morgan (1871), Macfarlane (1883) and Hobson (1894), produced work that embodied two of the features. Morgan collected huge amounts of systematic data on kinship and displayed his results in graphic images. Macfarlane developed an algebraic model of kinship and he too used graphic images to display its properties. Hobson collected systematic data on corporate interlocks, then drew hypergraphs to reveal their observed interlock patterns. By employing two of the four tools that define modern social network analysis, these nineteenth century investigators began to approach current practice.

From a network perspective, this chapter has raised some interesting issues. First, of all the people discussed here, only one, Georg Simmel, is generally recognized as having been influential in forming a foundation for social network analysis. Maine, Tönnies, Durkheim, Spencer, Cooley and von Wiese have been mentioned in the network literature, but rarely. There has been at least one citation to Hobson and one to Galton and Watson. This suggests that both works may have had some impact on the development of the field. But, as far as I can discover, even though their work could be expected to have influenced the development of the field, all the others I have discussed in this chapter are simply unknown in the social network community.

In any case, in the early 1930s a broad research effort called sociometry was introduced. It was the first work that included all four of the defining features of social network analysis. In the next chapter I will review its development.

Chapter 3

The Birth of Social Network Analysis I: Sociometry

Jacob Levy Moreno was the force behind the development of sociometry. He was an enigmatic figure. He was bright—perhaps brilliant—he was wildly creative, he was entertaining and he was blessed with boundless energy. Like many Viennese intellectuals of the early twentieth century he had presence and style. But, at the same time, Moreno had a dark side. He was self-centered, self-serving and by his own description, megalo-maniacal. He admitted hearing voices, he sometimes thought he was God and he was convinced that others were always stealing credit for ideas that were his. Moreno, then, was both a dynamic intellectual innovator and a severely troubled human being. His role in the development of social network analysis can be understood only by considering both facets of his personality.

At one level Moreno set out to create ambiguity. There are discrepant accounts of his life, beginning with his name and the circumstances of his birth. He was actually born in his parents' home in Bucharest on May 18, 1889, and he was originally given the name Jacob Levy. His biographer, Marineau (1989), has reproduced both his birth certificate (p. 7) and the register of his graduation from the faculty of medicine in Vienna (p. 8). Both documents indicate that he was born in 1889 and that his name was Jacob Levy, not Jacob Moreno.

But in his autobiography (1985, Ch. 1, p. 6) Jacob Moreno claimed to have been born in 1892 on the 400th anniversary of the forced exodus of Jews from Spain. He wrote:

> *I was born on a stormy night on a ship sailing the Black Sea from the Bosphorus to Constanta in Rou-mania. Dawn of the Holy Sabbath and the delivery took place just before the initial prayer. My being born on a ship was due to an honorable error, the excuse being that my mother was only sixteen and little ex-perienced in the mathematics of pregnancy. No one knew the identity of the ship's flag. Was she a Greek, a Turkish, a Roumanian or a Spanish ship? The ano-nymity of the ship's flag started off the anonymity of my name and the anonymity of my citizenship. When World War I broke out in 1914 no one knew whether I was a Turk, a Greek, a Roumanian, an Italian, or a Spaniard because I had no birth certificate…. I was born a citizen of the world.*

The fact is that Moreno was the eldest of six children born to Moreno Nissim Levy and his wife, Paulina Iancu. Moreno Levy was a Sephardic Jew and a relatively unsuccessful travel-ing salesman. Paulina was 15 years old — 17 years younger than her husband — when the marriage took place. She too was Sephardic, but she had been educated in a Catholic convent. So she ended up embracing both Jewish and Christian beliefs. As Marineau (1989, p. 13) put it, "Her hero, who was to become Jacob's model, was Jesus Christ."

Jacob was his mother's favorite, particularly after a gypsy reportedly advised her that "The day will come when this boy will become a very great man. People will come from all over the world to see him." His mother passed this tale around and it became the first of many stories that were later integrated into the legend that was created by the adult Moreno.

Another part of that legend was reported by Moreno him-self (1946, p. 2):

> *When I was four-and-a-half years old my parents lived in a house near the river Danube. They had left the*

house on a Sunday to pay a visit, leaving me alone in the basement of the house with the neighbors' children. The size of this basement was about three times that of an average room. It was empty except for a huge oak table in the middle. The children said, "Let's play." One child asked me: "What?" "I know", I said, "lets play God and his angels." The children inquired: "But who is God?" I replied "I am God and you are my angels." The children agreed. They all declared: "We must build the heavens first." We all dragged chairs from every room in the house to the basement, put them on the big table and began to build one heaven after another by tying several chairs together on one level and putting more chairs above them on the big table until we reached the ceiling. Then all the children helped me to climb up until I reached the top chair and sat on it. There I sat pretty. The children began to circle around the table, using their arms as wings, and singing. Suddenly, I heard a child asking me: "Why don't you fly?" I stretched my arms, trying it. A second later I fell and found myself on the floor, my right arm broken.

According to Marineau (1989, p. 17) this business of playing God was repeated often, and it was encouraged by Moreno's mother.

In the late 1890s the family moved to Vienna and young Jacob entered school. He was an excellent student, but when his parents separated he began to rebel. He dropped out of school, wore outlandish clothes and grew an unkempt full beard—unheard of in that period in Vienna. He took to hanging around the University of Vienna, and in 1909 he was finally admitted as a temporary student in philosophy. The following year he was able to transfer into the school of medicine. He received his medical degree in 1917 with a specialty in psychiatry.

After receiving his degree Moreno somewhat reluctantly started a medical practice. He moved to Bad Vöslau, a small town in Austria, where in 1920 he began a serious long-term relationship with a very beautiful young woman, Marianne Lörnitzo.

Moreno described Marianne as his "muse." Marineau (1989, p. 62) said that Marianne "…was instrumental (and perhaps the word is too weak) in making Moreno refocus…" In any case, with Marianne's influence, Moreno published two works: a long mystical poem, *Das Testament des Vaters* (The Words of the Father), and a rambling precursor of present day sociodrama and psychodrama, *Das Stegreiftheater* (The Theater of Spontaneity). These were the products of the first of a series of important encounters between Moreno and various women. For the most part Moreno seemed to be unfocused, but when he was involved with a woman—one who could serve as a "muse"—he succeeded in concentrating and was able to write.

In terms of social networks the most important aspect of this period in Moreno's life is that it includes a demonstration of his concern with social structure. *Das Stegreiftheater* contained his first sociometric diagrams. These show that, from his perspective, the therapeutic potential of drama stemmed from the interactions among the actors. As he (1953, p. xxxv) put it in a later description of *Das Stegreiftheater*:

> *Sociometric measurement started with things like this: how much "time" does an actor A spend with another actor B? He may spend half as much time with another actor C and three times as much time with another actor D. Or, what is the "spatial distance," near or far, in inches, feet or meters, between actors A, B, C and D in the course of the same situation and what effect have nearness or distance upon behavior and acting? Or, how frequently do two actors appear simultaneously in a scene and how frequently do they exit together?*

These kinds of structural intuitions are at the core of all of Moreno's work.

In any case, Moreno's career was not going well in Austria and at the end of 1925 he decided to emigrate to America. The plan was for Marianne to maintain their house in Bad Vöslau. He told her that he would send for her after he became established in the new world.

Moreno struggled learning English, but in 1927 he had developed enough skill to allow him to begin working with an impromptu theater group in New York. There, in 1928, he met and married Beatrice Beecher,[11] reportedly for the sole purpose of gaining American citizenship. He and Beecher were divorced, as they had agreed, in 1934 when Moreno did gain his citizenship. Interestingly, he never bothered to tell Marianne about this marriage. She still expected to join Moreno once he was established.

Most important from our present perspective, Moreno also made another new friend through the theater group, Helen Hall Jennings. At the time, Jennings was a graduate student in psychology at Columbia University. She worked with the prominent psychologist, Gardner Murphy, and specialized in research methods and statistics. She introduced Moreno to Murphy and helped him design and conduct sociometric studies at Sing Sing prison (Moreno, 1932) and at the Hudson School for Girls (Moreno, 1934). These two studies resulted in two books being published within two years. Both studies involved systematic data collection and analysis, and in his 1934 book he used the term "network" in the sense that it is used today. By the end of the Hudson study, the sociometric approach had been fully developed.

Moreno was listed as the sole author of these two books, although Jennings was credited with the authorship of a "supplement" in the 1934 volume. Nonetheless, his acknowledgements do include the phrase, "I and my collaborator, Helen Jennings,..." And in his autobiography he acknowledged her as a guiding force (Moreno, 1985, Ch. 3, p. 8).

It is impossible to overestimate the importance of Jennings in these works. Marineau (1989, p. 101) reports that "...it is fair to say that the work would have lacked precision and refinement without her help." Hare and Hare (1996, p. 73) describe her as having played "a major role in the collection and analysis of the data." And in his preface to her later book (Jennings, 1943) Gardner Murphy describes Jennings as "the initiator of many of the methods" of sociometry. In contrast to *Who Shall Survive?*

---

[11]She was the granddaughter of Henry Ward Beecher, the evangelist.

Jennings (1943) book, *Leadership and Isolation*, is far more organized and coherent. Homans (1984, p. 163) described it as "a much better book."

My own suspicion is that Jennings's contributions were immense. Moreno had no research training at all, and until this point, he had shown absolutely no interest in systematic research. All of his earlier publications were couched in heavy mysticism. But his newer works—those produced during his collaboration with Jennings—were comparatively systematic and were, for the first time, empirically grounded. The obvious conclusion is that, though the intuitive ideas came from Moreno, the completed research and the publications drew heavily on the contributions of Jennings. Jennings, it seems, was not only a collaborator but she was, in Moreno's terms, a very powerful "muse."

By the mid 1930s these books, along with public support from Jennings, Murphy and the prominent psychiatrist, William Allison White, turned Moreno into something of a social science celebrity. He started a journal, the *Sociometric Review*, in 1936. But a year later he dropped that publication and started another journal, *Sociometry*. By the late 1930s he could count among those who were involved in his work such notables as Franz Alexander, Gordon W. Allport, Read Bain, Howard Becker, Franz Boas, Emory S. Bogardus, Jerome S. Bruner, Hadley Cantril, F. Stuart Chapin, Leonard S. Cottrell, Stuart C. Dodd, Paul Lazarsfeld, Kurt Lewin, Charles P. Loomis, George A. Lundberg, Robert S. Lynd, Margaret Mead, Karl Menninger, George Peter Murdock, Gardner Murphy, Theodore M. Newcomb, William H. Sewell, Pitirim Sorokin and Samuel Stouffer. These names are a virtual *Who's Who* in American sociology and psychology at the time.

In a period in which most mainstream sociology had become psychologistic, it is remarkable that it took a psychiatrist, Moreno, and a psychologist, Jennings, to reintroduce a perspective that was distinctly structural. Like others at the time, Moreno and especially Jennings were concerned with psychological properties of individuals; they used sociometric questions to determine people's feelings about one another. They asked the members of a defined population to name the others with whom they would like to live, for example, or work or spend leisure time. The responses, then, were individual choices. But since the Moreno-Jennings approach used these choices to uncover groups and positions of individuals within those groups, their approach was essentially structural.

According to the *New York Times* (1933) Moreno first called his approach "psychological geography." But by 1934 he had renamed it *sociometry.* As Moreno (1934, pp. 10–11), described it, sociometry was based on an "...experimental technique...obtained by application of quantitative methods...which inquire into the evolution and organization of groups and the position of individuals within them."

This is certainly a structural concern, and one that falls at the very heart of social network analysis. A great deal of contemporary work is involved in the specification of both groups and positions. Examples of recent work on groups can be found in Alba (1973), Breiger (1974), Freeman, (1992), Mokken (1979), Winship (1977) and Yan (1988). Examples of work on positions can be found in reports by Breiger and Pattison (1986), Lorrain and White (1971), Sailer (1978), White and Reitz (1983) and Winship and Mandell (1983).

The question, then, is whether Moreno and his supporters exhibited all the features that define modern social network analysis. The Hares (1996, p. 30) reported that, "Moreno's theory of society focused on the networks of interpersonal relations that join individuals." That point is documented throughout Moreno's 1934 edition of *Who Shall Survive?* There, Moreno not only wrote explicitly about "networks," but he referred to "the effects beyond the two persons and the immediate group" of an interacting pair (p. 347). He (Moreno et al., 1960) illustrated the point by showing that an epidemic of runaways among the girls at the Hudson school could be explained by chains of social ties that linked all of those who had left. This is a clear and dramatic example of structural thinking.

The book includes systematic empirical data collected in a nursery, several classrooms and the cottages and work groups in the Hudson school for girls. Graphics were used throughout. An example, shown in Figure 3.1, shows the positive and negative sociometric choices made by members of a football team (p. 213).

There was one defining element of contemporary social network analysis, however, that was missing in these two books. The 1932 and 1934 volumes included no mathematical or com-

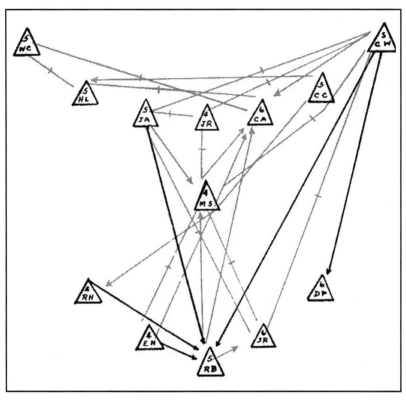

Figure 3.1. Sociogram of a football team

putational models at all. But Moreno (or, more likely, Jennings) soon recognized that deficiency and enlisted the help of the eminent mathematical sociologist at Columbia, Paul Lazarsfeld. In response, Lazarsfeld created a base-line model for sociometric choice. Given random choices, he worked out the probability that any particular individual would be chosen by any other particular individual. Moreno and Jennings then published Lazarsfeld's model in an article in volume 1, number 2 of the new journal *Sociometry* (1938, pp. 342–374). According to Nehnevajsa (1956), the Lazarsfeld model "...stands at the roots of probabilistic analysis in the field."

By 1938, then, the work of Moreno—with the help of Jennings and Lazarsfeld—had displayed all four of the features that define contemporary social network analysis. It is clear, moreover, that they recognized the generality of their approach. They collected data on positive and negative emotional choices and on who was acquainted with whom. They observed interaction patterns linking individuals. They discussed kinship ties. And they examined social roles. As Moreno (1937) put it:

> *The first decisive step in the development of Sociometry was the disclosure of the actual organization of the group. The second decisive step was the inclusion of subjective measures in determining this organization. The third decisive step was a method which gives to subjective terms the highest possible degree of objectivity, through the function of the auxiliary ego. The fourth decisive step was the consideration of the criterion (a need, a value, an aim, etc.) around which a particular structure develops.*

Every one of these steps was focused on the structural patterning of the data.

Clearly, with a great deal of help from Jennings and Lazarsfeld, Moreno had developed an approach that included all of the defining properties of social network analysis. It was based on structural intuitions, it involved the collection of systematic empirical data, graphic imagery was an integral part of its tools and it embodied an explicit mathematical model. That structural perspective, moreover, was generalized to a range of phenomena. Thus, the group led by Moreno displayed all four of the features that define social network analysis.

At this point, sociometry had the attention of the elite of the American social science community. So the question is, why didn't the sociometric model of the social network approach take off after the late 1930s? What led to the marginalization of sociometry and the necessity for the reintroduction of social network analysis at a later time?

The answer, I think, can be found in the other aspect—the dark side—of Moreno's character. For a brief period Jennings was able to "clean up his act" and present him to the world as a creative social scientist who was capable of conducting systematic research. But she was unable to suppress the fundamental flaws in his character. So although Jennings introduced us to Moreno as Dr. Jeckyll, as time went on, Mr. Hyde kept reappearing.

During his university years Moreno (1985, Ch. 1, p. 2) confessed, "I began to believe that I was an extraordinary person, that I was here on the planet to fulfill an extraordinary mission." So as a student he formed a new religion, became its one prophet and began to gather disciples. By 1920 he reported hearing voices—both as a child and as an adult. But he hastened to add that that he didn't hear voices "…as a mental patient does."

He went on to claim that he experienced "direct encounters with God" (Hare and Hare, 1996, p. 26). And, he insisted, he often "played" God. In particular, he played God with his second wife. In 1938, Moreno had married a Columbia student named Florence Bridge. She apparently adored her husband and she encouraged his God playing. But despite her adoration, it turned out that Bridge was unsatisfactory as a "muse."

In 1941, when he met another beautiful young woman, Celine Zerka Toeman, he finally found the "integrated partner" he had been seeking. He married Zerka in 1949, and according to Marineau (1989, p. 107):

> Zerka was his partner in all his publications, conferences, workshops, and many other ventures. There is no doubt that she was not only his inspiration, but also full-time administrator, organizer, co-trainer and co-therapist.

Zerka particularly supported Moreno's ideas about therapy, and the two of them began to put increasing effort into the development of group psychotherapy, psychodrama and sociodrama as therapeutic techniques. Thus, by the end of the 1940s,

Moreno had quit making contributions to sociometry and turned his attention almost completely to various forms of therapy.

In 1953, however, Moreno did publish a second edition of his 1934 book, Who Shall Survive? That book embodied several new sections, including in its first 100 pages his "Preludes to the sociometric movement." These preludes take the form of a long rambling narrative. In it he referred often to God. He laid claim to having originated virtually every important idea in social science. He demeaned the contributions of others including Marx and Freud. And he finally wound up with several pages of diatribe condemning Kurt Lewin and especially Lewin's students, whom he accused of having a problem "of *interpersonal ethics*."[12] He laid particular blame on Ronald Lippitt, Alvin Zander, John R. P. French, Alex Bavelas, Leland P. Bradford, C. Hendry, Margaret Barron and Kenneth D. Benne. He accused these and other students of Lewin of crediting Lewin for ideas they learned while attending Moreno's workshops. As he put it, they used "a technique of quoting only each other, that is, those who belong to their clique, and not quoting any of my close associates or myself."

Moreno's increasing preoccupation with therapeutic procedures, along with his apparent abandonment of systematic sociometric work, tended to drive many early supporters away. For those who were interested in empirically based structural research, the attraction of the sociometric paradigm was dulled by Moreno's insistence that sociometry had to do, not with structural research, but with ambiguous links to God and to psychotherapy. Then too, his increasing megalomania put people off. The kinds of statements described above led research-oriented scholars to have serious misgivings about the whole sociometric enterprise. In fact, it is reasonable to conjecture that the unwillingness of the Lewin students to associate their names with Moreno was, for the most part, a consequence of his own bizarre behavior.

My own memories of Moreno date from the 1950s when he was still presenting his work at annual sociology meetings. Those

---

[12]Italics in the original.

presentations always took the form of demonstrations of impromptu theater. His style was bombastic and overbearing but his theater was always entertaining. Although Moreno's dramas might have provided entertainment, they seemed to me to lack serious intellectual content—they failed to cast any light on sociological questions.

My reactions were not unique. Moreno's work attracted ever fewer sociological followers. After 1955 Moreno turned his journal, *Sociometry*, over to the (then) American Sociological Society, and it became a general social psychology journal (renamed *Social Psychology Quarterly*). As the years went by, the earlier romance between sociology and sociometry faded completely (Hare and Hare, 1996, p. 107).

Jacob Moreno, then, was—at least for a short time—a major intellectual force. With support from various allies he defined an approach that contained all the features of modern social network analysis. And in the 1930s and 40s he succeeded in attracting the interest of most of the major figures in empirical social research.

But his commitment to mysticism, his bombastic personal style and his megalomania drove most of his early supporters away. These features of Moreno's persona were too much for regular members of the academic community to bear. They simply could not be accommodated in the day-to-day academic or scientific world. As his biographer Marineau (1989, p. 121) put it, "Very few young students of sociology or social psychology today would ever have suspected the impact that Moreno had on this field of research and practice more than fifty years ago."

So in the field of sociometry, the techniques of contemporary social network analysis were developed and then abandoned. Most people simply backed off from Moreno the man, and in so doing they refused to recognize the importance and generality of Moreno's approach. Social research, then, continued to lack a unified structural paradigm. In the next chapter I will describe another attempt to provide such a paradigm.

Chapter 4

The Birth of Social Network Analysis II: The First Harvard Thrust

A research effort that focused on the study of social structure began at Harvard in the late 1920s. Centered in the Graduate School of Business Administration on one side of the Charles River and the Society of Fellows on the other, it involved a relatively large number of faculty, including William Lloyd Warner, George Elton Mayo, Fritz Roethlisberger, T. North Whitehead and Lawrence J. Henderson. A number of students from a variety of disciplines were also involved, including Eliot Chapple, Conrad Arensberg, Allison Davis, Elizabeth Davis, Burleigh Gardner, George Caspar Homans and William Foote Whyte.

The main intellectual thrust for the study of social structure at Harvard came from Warner (shown in Figure 4.1), who called himself "W. Lloyd Warner." Warner was born in Colton, California in 1898.[13] After high school, he started college at the University of Southern California. But after his freshman year he transferred to the University of California, Berkeley, where he majored in English. Although in 1923 he dropped out and spent a year working in New York and acting on Broadway[14],

---

[13]Both Collins (1994) and Scott (2000, p. 16) have incorrectly characterized Warner as Australian.

[14]He had a walk-on part in the George Arliss play, *The Green Goddess* (Warner, 1988, p.10).

43

the following year he returned to Berkeley. With the help of the anthropologist Robert Lowie he was readmitted to the university.

Having gained Lowie's support, Warner switched to anthropology and received his B.A. in that field in 1925. He entered graduate school at Berkeley and worked with Lowie and with the British anthropologist Bronislaw Malinowski who was visiting in the Berkeley department. But then another British visitor arrived for a brief stay. Alfred Reginald Radcliffe-Brown stopped in at Berkeley en route from Oxford to a new position at the University of Sydney.

During his Berkeley stay, Radcliffe-Brown attended a dinner put on by the Anthropology Club. At one point in the proceedings, he called across the table, "I say, Warner, how would you like to come to Australia with me?" Warner gave a joking reply, but Radcliffe-Brown convinced him that the offer was genuine, and Warner accepted it. Radcliff-Brown sent him off to Harvard for a short stay so that he could learn something about

physical anthropology from Ernest Hooton. Then Warner sailed to Australia, arriving in Sydney in January of 1927. After a little more preliminary training, Radcliffe-Brown sent him out to the bush to do field work.

Warner worked among the Murngin for more than two years. He collected ethnographic data, and following a suggestion by Radcliffe-Brown, he concentrated particularly on determining their kinship patterns and rules of descent (Warner, 1937).

Figure 4.1. W. Lloyd Warner, circa 1920s

Then, in 1929, again with Radcliffe-Brown's support, he returned to Harvard, this time as an Instructor in anthropology and a Tutor at Kirkland House.

Even before leaving Australia, Warner had described to Radcliffe-Brown his desire to use ethnographic field methods in the study of industrial communities (Warner, 1988, p. 41). And once he got to Harvard, he immediately set out to do just that. He chose the relatively small industrial city of Newburyport, Massachusetts, as a study site, and recruited a collection of Harvard graduate and undergraduate students to collect data. An undergraduate senior, Eliot Chapple, was appointed field director. Others involved included a married couple, Allison and Elizabeth (Liddy) Davis, Conrad Arensberg, Solon (Sol) Kimball, Leo Srole, Buford Junker, J. O. Low, Paul Lunt and Burleigh Gardner.

The "Yankee City" study, as it was called, focused primarily on the study of stratification. The orientation of the research was influenced by Durkheim (Warner and Lunt, 1941, p. 10), and by Simmel (pp. 12–13). It centered on studying interaction among individuals (Warner and Lunt, 1941, p. 12):

> *Throughout our research we have employed the concepts of interaction between two or more individuals and the social interrelationships within which these interactions take place. The explicit, overt behavior of individuals, verbally or bodily, as well as "mental attitudes or psychological occurrences within the minds of the individuals" studied, have been understood by us "as a product of mutual determinations and reciprocal influences."…The larger systems of interrelations which compose the extremely complex and highly elaborate society of Yankee City were studied in specific detail, as were the interactions, direct and indirect, of the individuals who constituted the biological units of the group.*

Thus, the focus of this research was on interpersonal networks. Moreover, over a period of data collection that lasted several years, as many as a dozen graduate students (Warner, 1988,

p. 86), produced "literally tons" of empirical data (Roethlisberger, 1977, p. 55). And, throughout the report, graphic images were employed. Figure 4.2 is a diagram of an idealized version of the

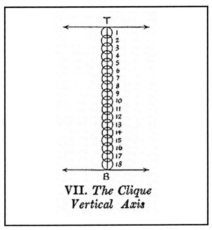

Figure 4.2. An idealized model of overlapping "cliques"[15]

hierarchical organization of overlapping cliques where the vertical dimension is social status (Warner and Lunt, 1941)

Warner's organization of the Yankee City project, however, was just the beginning of his contribution to spreading the gospel of structural analysis at Harvard. Almost immediately upon his arrival he met George Elton Mayo (known simply as Elton Mayo). Mayo was from Australia. He had trained in medicine, but quit before he received his degree. Instead, he switched to psychology and received a bachelor's degree from the University of Queensland. Mayo taught at Queensland until 1922, when he migrated to the United States. He was supported by a Rockefeller grant and went to work at the Wharton (business) School of the University of Pennsylvania doing industrial research. In 1926 he accepted an appointment in the Harvard Business School.

By the time Mayo got to Harvard, engineers and personnel managers at the Western Electric Corporation in Cicero, Illinois, were already deeply involved in the first major research studying industrial productivity. Western Electric was at that time a

---

[15]This research was conduced before Luce and Perry (1949) formally defined cliques. The term "clique" was used in the Yankee City study in an informal intuitive sense.

subsidiary of the Bell Telephone Company, responsible for the manufacture of telephones and phone equipment. The project had begun in 1924. It grew out of an attempt to determine the degree to which the use of artificial lighting might affect worker productivity on the production line (Gillespie, 1991, p. 38). The electrical industry encouraged Western Electric to do the study in the hope that with the use of electric lights productivity would rise and industry would, therefore, be encouraged to consume more power. But from the perspective of the electrical industry, the early results were bad. They showed that lighting had little if any effect on productivity. The type of supervision, it turned out, was a far more important factor.

In 1927 the director of the Western Electric research, George Pennock, attended a lecture by Elton Mayo. Pennock was anxious to extend the research into new areas and he was impressed with Mayo's talents. So, beginning in 1928, Western Electric enlisted Mayo's participation in their research effort. Adams and Butler (2000, p. 126) described Mayo's first visit to the Western Electric plant:

> *The company put him up at a Chicago landmark, the Palmer House hotel, where he was extended the same courtesy (or privilege) as Hawthorne Works manager C. L. Rice. A bemused Mayo wrote his wife: "Every morning at 8:30 the doorman clears the taxis away from the Wabash St. entrance of the hotel —-and a large limousine with a uniformed chauffer slides noiselessly in. The door is opened and Elton Mayo, formerly of South Australia, gets in and glides off to his alleged industrial researches."*

Once established, Mayo changed the focus of the Western Electric research. The earlier investigations had examined the effects of lighting and other physical interventions on productivity. As an alternative, Mayo suggested concentrating on the effects of the psychological characteristics of the workers on their productivity. He put together a team from the Harvard Graduate School of Business Administration. The Harvard team included T. North Whitehead[16] and one of Mayo's earlier students, Fritz Jules Roethlisberger. These two worked on the project along with Mayo and two Western Electric employees, William Dickson and Harold Wright.[17]

In 1930, Mayo recruited Warner as a half-time member of the Business School faculty and as an advisor to the Western Electric project. Warner's (1988, p. 45) perspective on the research was expressed in an early memo to Mayo:

> *An important problem before us at the present time in the Western Electric research is to study and understand the total social organization of each of the test rooms. This includes not only the formal industrial structure which the company has created but also the organizations formed by the employees in their conscious or unconscious attempts to form themselves into a group of their own....The first step necessary is to itemize the number of social personalities found in each place—by this I mean the types of occupations performed by the workers found in the two test rooms.... All of these social personalities are integrated by a set of primary and secondary relationships which can be analyzed into separate parts. [Sixteen categories are listed]...Following the analysis of the social situation into its primary reciprocals, it will be necessary then to combine the various reciprocals into secondary association to see how these various social bonds react on each other and finally to integrate the social situation in the test rooms on the basis of social relationships which exist there.*

From this statement it is clear that, by then, Warner had fully embraced a structural perspective. In it he stressed examining the patterning of the informal ties among the workers, and

---

[16]T. North was a faculty member in the Harvard Business School. He was the son of the eminent philosopher, Alfred North Whitehead. Both Whiteheads were at that time teaching at Harvard.

[17]Mayo's research was famous for producing the "Hawthorne effect" in which the mere presence of observers seemed to enhance worker productivity.

that kind of emphasis on studying informal links is still found in contemporary social network analysis. His notion of "secondary reciprocals" undoubtedly came from his earlier research on Murngin kinship in Australia, designed to call attention to the implications of social ties for one another. Both of these ideas expressed particularly sophisticated views for the period.

Mayo got the message. He was convinced that Warner's proposed focus on the social aspects of behavior was important. He (Mayo, 1933, pp. 116–117) later reported his reaction to Warner's views:

> *A representative of the Harvard Department of Anthropology had called attention to the logical insufficiency of a merely psychological study of the individuals in the department (the wiring room). Laboratory and clinical psychological studies are interested in the individual...but they do no more than touch the fringe of human inquiry.*

Consequently, because of Warner's input to the Western Electric project, the research deviated from Mayo's strict psychological focus on individual characteristics; instead, it focused on social structure. The result was a study of the patterning of interaction among the workers in the bank wiring room. That research was described in detail by Roethlisberger and Dickson (1939) in their book, *Management and the Worker*.

Following Warner's suggestion, data on interpersonal interaction were collected using systematic observation. An observer was placed in the workroom. He recorded six different kinds of interpersonal links: (1) who played games with whom, (2) who engaged in controversies with whom, (3) who traded jobs with whom, (4) who helped whom, (5) who displayed friendly behavior toward whom and (6) who was antagonistic toward whom. Since it was based on systematic observation of links among individuals, the bank wiring room study generated social network data. These data were reviewed by Mayo, Roethlisberger, T. N. Whitehead, Warner and George Homans along with several Western Electric Executives (Roethlisberger, 1977, p. 49).

But in addition to structural intuitions and systematic data on social links, this research also generated graphic images of network ties. The patterning of each of the social ties was dis-

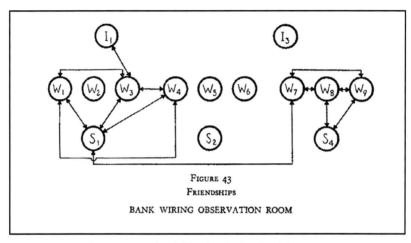

Figure 4.3. Friendships in the bank wiring room

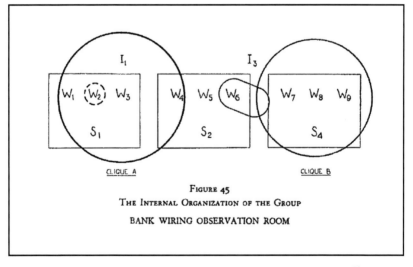

Figure 4.4. Reported "cliques" in the bank wiring room[18]

---

[18]See footnote 15 above.

played using directed graphs, and a generalized overall "clique" structure was produced in the form of a hypergraph. These features are reproduced in Figures 4.3 and 4.4.

Overall, then, the bank wiring room research was quite sophisticated in its approach. It embodied three of the four elements found in current social network research. It missed only by not including any mathematical or computational tools. But in every other respect it came very close to the contemporary standard.

In 1933 Warner continued his research on stratification by organizing the "Deep South" project. Deep South was a study of the impact of race differences on social stratification that was conducted in Natchez Mississippi. Natchez was chosen because it was roughly the same size as Newburyport and it was a totally segregated city with a large black population.

Warner chose a black couple, Allison and Elizabeth Davis, and a white couple, Burleigh and Mary Gardner, to settle down in Nachez and do fieldwork in the black and the white communities. Then Allison Davis recruited my own undergraduate mentor and his former undergraduate student, St. Clair Drake, to help in the collection and analysis of the data in the black community.[19] Davis and Drake are pictured in Figures 4.5 and 4.6 respectively. Their effort, along with that of the Gardners, produced a book titled *Deep South* (Davis, Gardner and Gardner, 1941).

As in the Yankee City research, Davis, Gardner and Gardner were

Figure 4.5. Allison Davis honored on a U.S. postage stamp

concerned with the question of the degree to which members of various social classes limited their interaction to others at ap-

---

[19] The rumor was that Davis turned out to be uncomfortable interviewing lower class informants and recruited Drake to do that job.

Figure 4.6. St. Clair Drake

proximately the same social class level. To find out, they recorded the observed patterns of interaction that linked collections of
individuals. They set out to specify the "clique" memberships
of individuals in terms of who interacted with whom. They collected systematic two-mode network data on co-attendance
among a collection of eighteen white women. These data are
shown in Figure 4.7. And with the help of Drake they collected
similar data linking black males and produced structural imag-

Names of Participants of Group I	Code Numbers and Dates of Social Events Reported in *Old City Herald*													
	(1) 6/27	(2) 3/2	(3) 4/12	(4) 9/26	(5) 2/25	(6) 5/19	(7) 3/15	(8) 9/16	(9) 4/8	(10) 6/10	(11) 2/23	(12) 4/7	(13) 11/21	(14) 8/3
1. Mrs. Evelyn Jefferson	×	×	×	×	×	×	....	×	×	....	....	....	....	....
2. Miss Laura Mandeville	×	×	×	....	×	×	×	×	....	....	....	....	....	....
3. Miss Theresa Anderson	....	×	×	×	×	×	×	×	×	....	....	....	....	....
4. Miss Brenda Rogers	×	....	×	×	×	×	×	×	....	....	....	....	....	....
5. Miss Charlotte McDowd	....	....	×	×	×	....	×	....	....	....	....	....	....	....
6. Miss Frances Anderson	....	....	×	....	×	×	....	×	....	....	....	....	....	....
7. Miss Eleanor Nye	....	....	....	....	×	×	×	×	....	....	....	....	....	....
8. Miss Pearl Oglethorpe	....	....	....	....	....	×	....	×	×	....	....	....	....	....
9. Miss Ruth DeSand	....	....	....	....	×	....	×	×	×	....	....	....	....	....
10. Miss Verne Sanderson	....	....	....	....	....	....	×	×	×	....	....	×	....	....
11. Miss Myra Liddell	....	....	....	....	....	....	....	×	×	×	....	×	....	....
12. Miss Katherine Rogers	....	....	....	....	....	....	....	×	×	×	....	×	×	×
13. Mrs. Sylvia Avondale	....	....	....	....	....	....	×	×	×	×	....	×	×	×
14. Mrs. Nora Fayette	....	....	....	....	....	×	×	....	×	×	×	×	×	×
15. Mrs. Helen Lloyd	....	....	....	....	....	....	×	×	....	×	×	×	....	....
16. Mrs. Dorothy Murchison	....	....	....	....	....	....	....	×	×	....	....	....	....	....
17. Mrs. Olivia Carleton	....	....	....	....	....	....	....	....	×	....	×	....	....	....
18. Mrs. Flora Price	....	....	....	....	....	....	....	....	×	....	×	....	....	....

Fig. 3.—Frequency of interparticipation of a group of women in Old City, 1936—Group I.

Figure 4.7. Attendance of 18 women at 14 social events

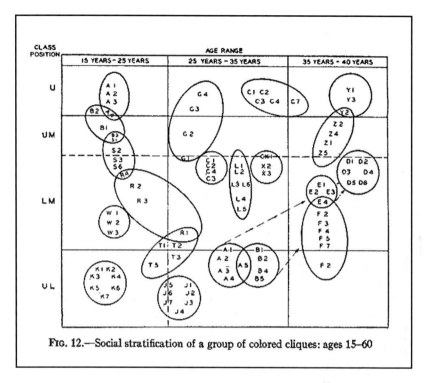

FIG. 12.—Social stratification of a group of colored cliques: ages 15–60

Figure 4.8. "Clique" memberships of males[20]

es in the form of hypergraphs showing "clique" memberships (see Figure 4.8).

The Davis, Gardner and Gardner report, then, displayed the same structural perspective that was present in all of the work by Warner and his students. They were motivated by structural ideas, they collected systematic who-to-whom data and they used graphic images to display their results. But nowhere in any of this early work is there any use of mathematical or computational tools.

During this period Warner organized regular seminars at Harvard that aimed at organizing and coordinating these community-study projects. The seminars were attended by those faculty members who were involved in the Western Electric research: Elton Mayo, T. North Whitehead and Fritz Roethlisberg-

---

[20]See footnote 3 above.

er. Another frequent attendee was Lawrence Joseph Henderson of the Business School.

At that time, Henderson was a major figure at Harvard. He was a direct descendant of an old-line family in Salem, Massachusetts. He had attended Harvard College and the Harvard Medical School where he earned an M.D. degree. He went to work at Harvard where he became a prominent professor of biological chemistry. His work on blood chemistry was recognized throughout the world. Henderson was, moreover, a close personal friend of the Harvard President, A. Lawrence Lowell.[21]

Henderson had been teaching in the College of Arts and Science, not only in biological chemistry but in philosophy and the history of science as well. In 1927 he shocked the Harvard community when he moved across the Charles River and joined the faculty of the Graduate School of Business Administration. Henderson, it seems, had very wide interests.

Along with Alfred North Whitehead, Henderson was troubled by the limitations in standard graduate education. They got together with some colleagues and proposed that Harvard develop a system of fellowships. Their idea was that a few Senior Fellows could guide the work of a small number of outstandingly talented Junior Fellows. This would free up the Junior Fellows from the usual dull routine of graduate study, examinations and the like, and allow them to pursue their own interests—wherever those interests might lead.

In 1932 President Lowell instituted and personally funded the plan. He appointed Henderson as its first chairman. At that time Henderson was excited about sociology, or rather, the sociology of the Italian economist, Vilfredo Pareto. A colleague from entomology, William Wheeler, had just suggested that Henderson read Pareto's work. Henderson was so completely taken with Pareto's sociological views (1916/1963) that he introduced a seminar on Pareto that continued for several years.

Despite his achievements in economics, Pareto's (1916/1963) sociology is made up almost entirely of psychobabble. For the most part he tried to account for the existence of various—often

---

[21] Harvard at the time was still dominated by the old Massachusetts aristocracy. A. Lawrence Lowell was one of *the* Lowells who, as the saying goes, "speak only to God."

questionable—"social facts" in terms of a complex collection of presumed cognitive characteristics of individuals. Pareto's "social facts" included, for example, the fact that people are able to choose numbers in lotteries. Their choice is "explained by the human instinct for combinations" (p. 516). Moreover the fact that people intone religious chants is a result of their "need of expressing sentiments by external acts" (p. 517).

Notwithstanding the intellectual poverty of Pareto's sociology, Henderson's seminar attracted a stellar collection of participants. They included the Business School faculty: Warner, Mayo, Roethlisberger and T. North Whitehead. And they also brought in Joseph Schumpeter, Crane Brinton, Bernard DeVoto, Charles Curtis, Hans Zinzer, Talcott Parsons, Kingsley Davis, Robert Merton and for a brief period, the chairman of Harvard's Sociology Department, Pitirim Sorokin. Most important in the present context, Henderson hired a recent Harvard graduate, a young aspiring poet, George Caspar Homans, as the seminar's administrator. This was Homans' first introduction to sociology.

Homans reaction to that seminar is documented by the fact that it led to his first book, written with Charles Curtis (1934). That book was simply the presentation of Pareto's ideas written for an American audience. Homans' lifelong focus on interaction and sentiments, moreover, turns out to have been inspired by Pareto (1916/1963, p. 614):

> *Whatever the causes, groups came to be formed among many peoples. Presumably they were bound to the soil and endured in time, the dead being one by one replaced by successors. It also happened that the nucleus of such groups was constituted by individuals bound to one another by ties of kinship. The existence of such groups stands in a relationship of interdependence with the existence of sentiments tending to make the groups permanent…*

Homans, shown in Figure 4.9, was born in 1910 to a wealthy old-line Boston family. In fact, his mother was an Adams. Like Lowell and Henderson, then, Homans was a Boston Brahmin—and quite proud of it. At one point, according to John Barnes,

Homans had been talking about American society with the prominent Indian sociologist, M. N. Srinivas. After listening to Homans' views, Srinivas—who was a Brahmin—accused

Figure 4.9. George Caspar Homans

Homans of presenting a Brahmin view of American society. Homans thought for a moment, and then replied, "Yes, by God, I'm a true Boston Brahmin."

True to his Brahmin heritage, Homans had attended St. Paul's preparatory school and then enrolled at Harvard. He received his bachelor's degree in 1932. His field was poetry. But his work with the Pareto seminar led to a change in direction.

In 1934 Homans was chosen as a Junior Fellow in the Harvard Society of Fellows and he remained in that position until 1939. Junior Fellows were expected to work with Senior Fellows and Homans worked primarily with L. J. Henderson. And, at Henderson's urging, he also worked extensively with Elton Mayo.

Fortunately for Homans, Mayo insisted that he read some social science beyond Pareto. Mayo introduced him to a good deal of the literature in psychology as well as to the works of the anthropologists Malinowski and Radcliffe-Brown (Homans, 1984, pp. 135–166). Moreover, Homans' association with Henderson and Mayo—both Business School faculty—led him to meet Warner. Through that contact, Homans met and became friends with two of Warner's students, Eliot Chapple and Conrad Arensberg. Both were influential on his thinking. Although Arensberg introduced Homans to Moreno's ideas (Homans, 1984, p. 163), and this led Homans to cite Moreno favorably in his later work (Homans, 1950, pp. 40–42), there is no indication that Moreno had much effect on his intellectual development.

Finally, in 1939 Sorokin, who was the Chairman of the Sociology Department at Harvard, hired Homans as an instructor. Although he was never particularly close to Sorokin, Homans speculated that he was hired because he had resisted the lure of Parsons' "fuzzy thought" and "sloppy writing" (Tilly, 1989). At Harvard, Homans worked his way up from Instructor until he was appointed Professor in 1953. In that year he visited Britain and taught at Manchester University. In subsequent years he went to Cambridge where he received his highest degree, an M.A., in 1955. He returned to his job at Harvard in 1956.

While he was still a Fellow, Homans began to develop what he (Homans, 1984, p. 164) called his "threefold classification." He proposed that interaction frequency, sentiment and joint activity (first called "function") are all interrelated. This idea was first introduced in print in the last chapter of his book on thirteenth century English village life (Homans, 1941). There (p. 405) he went on to suggest that:

> ...it is possible to observe that the action of one man is a stimulus for the action of a second, and that this action of the second is in turn a stimulus for the action of the first. Or the action of the second becomes a stimulus for the action of a third, and so forth. We have seen that a society can be defined as any group of people interacting in this way. Within a society so defined, the chains of interaction are infinitely com-

plex and cover the society in a number of different ways.

These remarks capture the essence of social network analysis. And his early ideas on the threefold classification provided a précis of his much more ambitious volume, *The Human Group* (Homans, 1950). In that book he developed and refined his classification and showed how it might help to explain some structural phenomena.

Specifically, *The Human Group* focused on showing how the structure of groups and the positions of individuals in those groups might emerge from the interrelations among his three variables. He examined structural data that others (including his colleagues at Harvard, Davis, Gardner, and Gardner (1940), Roethlisberger and Dickson (1939) and William Foote Whyte (1943) had collected. Moreover, he reproduced images of graphs and hypergraphs from Roethlisberger and Dickson. But, like the Hawthorne group, the Yankee City group and the Deep South group, Homans simply failed to develop or to draw upon any mathematical or computational tools.

This failure might be surprising since his mentor, Henderson, had insisted that Homans learn some mathematics during his years as a junior fellow (Homans, 1984, p. 122). Unfortunately, Henderson made Homans read the calculus rather than exposing him to algebra or probability theory. The result was that Homans' mathematical training was entirely inappropriate for his chosen work. The calculus could not provide any useful tools for refining his ideas about social structure.

William Foote Whyte and Conrad Arensberg were added to the collection of Junior Fellows in 1936. By that time, Arensberg had a great deal of experience at Harvard, and he took the new Harvard student, Whyte, under his wing. Whyte's undergraduate degree from Swarthmore was in economics. He had planned to continue in economics at Harvard when he arrived there, but Chapple and particularly Arensberg convinced him that he should focus on studying social structure (Whyte, 1994, p. 63; 1997, pp. 19–20). For that study, he chose a slum community in Boston's North End that he called "Cornerville." He entered that community as a participant observer and came out with a classic book, *Street Corner Society* (1943).

Whyte's book contains no systematic data, but it is rich in ethnographic detail. Its aim was to detail the social structure of the community by observing interaction patterns among its citizens, and it provides a full description of that structure. It includes graphic images, like the one reproduced in Figure 4.10, that are designed to depict structural arrangements. This work, then, is clearly in line with the whole structural thrust at Harvard in the 1930s. Though it lacked systematic data and it did not use mathematical tools, it did lay out the structural form of the interaction patterns linking individuals.

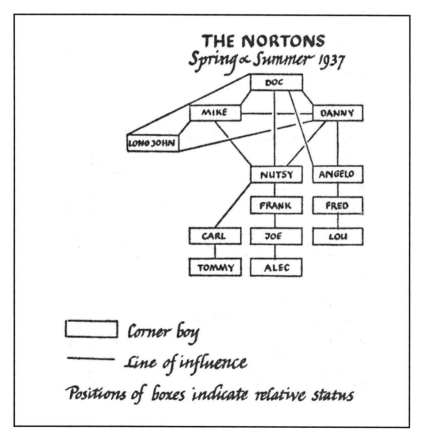

Figure 4.10. Whyte's image of the Nortons

By the mid-1930s, then, the efforts at Harvard had come close, but had never included all four of the features that define social network analysis. Structural intuitions dominated all of this work. Two of the projects, the Western Electric research and the Deep South study, produced systematic relational data. All of it also drew on visual images. But none of the work described so far developed or used any mathematical or computational tools.

Chapple and Arensberg, however, moved to fill that gap. They had returned from collecting data on the Yankee City project somewhat disillusioned. As Homans (1984, p. 162) reported, "What came to bother Chapple and later Arensberg was the lack of rigor with which the results of social research could be made and reported." So they set themselves the task of providing a framework for the systematic collection and analysis of structural data. As Whyte (1994, p. 63) described it:

> Their framework was designed to focus on objectively observable behavior, thus bypassing the subjectivity inherent in methods that focused on the interpretation of what people say. Arensberg argued that, whenever the same individuals interact over a period of time, a structure for that interaction emerges. That structure can be determined through direct observation, and that structure will strongly influence what people say, think, feel, and do.

They began to develop a rigorous operational definition of the variable "interaction." Chapple (Chapple, 1940) devised a "recording typewriter" to collect carefully timed data on the interaction pattern linking a pair of individuals. And although he had agreed to work with Warner on the analyses of the Yankee City data, he backed down. Warner's wife, Mildred Warner (1988, p. 121), described Chapple's withdrawal:

> …he had developed a system of analysis inconsistent with that used in the research, indeed, inconsistent with the purposes for which the research material had been gathered, and he felt that he could not meet his commitment since his report would conflict with oth-

> *ers. His primary interest had become a system of quan-*
> *titative analysis on which he and Conrad Arensberg*
> *were working.*

In any case, Chapple and Arensberg developed ways to collect and analyze detailed data about social linkages. As a part of that effort, they (Chapple, 1940, p. 79) faced a problem:

> *I order to describe a system of relations quantitative-*
> *ly, it is necessary to deal with a large number of rela-*
> *tions simultaneously. Otherwise we have to take each*
> *individual in turn and work out the equations describ-*
> *ing his relations, with no way of synthesizing the sys-*
> *tem as a whole.*

To solve that problem, they consulted with Harvard mathematician, Willard Quine. With Quine's help they developed an algebraic model generalized from kinship. They defined unit relations (foreman to worker or father to daughter) and calculated relative products (foreman to daughter of worker) and their inverses (woman to foreman in father's department). They organized these concatenations into matrices in order to deal with large sets of compound relations.

Quine, Chapple and Arensberg, then, provided the missing feature. Following their contribution, the Harvard group displayed all of the features of contemporary social network analysis. Unfortunately these efforts did not result in the emergence of a recognized "school" of structural analysis. Indeed, almost immediately after Chapple and Arensberg introduced their formal model, the collective effort was abandoned.

Warner, Gardner, Davis and Drake all left for the University of Chicago in 1935. Following Arensberg's advice to go study with Warner, in 1940 Whyte followed them to Chicago, where he completed his PhD. Gardner also completed his PhD at Chicago. Then he started a market research firm and recruited Warner as an active partner in that effort. Davis, Drake and, later, Whyte also completed their PhDs at Chicago. Afterwards Davis accepted an appointment in Chicago's Department of Education. Drake specialized in black studies and went to work first at Roosevelt College and finally at Stanford. Whyte decided that he would rather work with Everett C. Hughes in Chicago's Sociology Department than with Warner in Anthropology. He followed Hughes' lead and devoted the rest of his career to participant observation in various settings. He wound up teaching at Cornell. Chapple completed his PhD at Harvard and was appointed to a faculty position in Sociology and in the Harvard Business School. He soon quit, however, to become a consultant to industry. Arensberg took a position at the Massachusetts Institute of Technology in 1934 and from there went on to Columbia in 1946 where he remained until his retirement.

Henderson died in 1942. Mayo retired in 1947. And, according to Roethlisberger (1977, p. 308) the previously unified Harvard approach to the study "human relations" had, by then, divided into two parts: (1) the "case method" associated with Mayo and Roethlisberger's own work, and (2) the "applied anthropology" approach associated with Chapple, Arensberg and Whyte. Since Whyte took a very different tack than Chapple and Arensberg, Roethlisberger's grouping them all together is difficult to understand., Roethlisberger (1977, p. 57) was apparently troubled by the rigor and formalism of Chapple and Arensberg's work:

> Eliot's "breakthrough" seemed to me to be a "break with" a more pedestrian approach. The development of the social sciences, it seemed to me, would require for a long time just ordinary "tillers of the soil" (clinicians and field workers), not fancy "new models." In this sense Eliot was a threat to the development of the area as I thought it should take place at the Business School....So Eliot had me disturbed plenty; my emerging career at the Business School, as I then envisaged it, was at stake.

At the same time, Whyte (1994, p. 63), whom Roethlisberger had grouped together with Chapple and Arensberg, also objected to their approach:

> Impressed as I was with the micromeasurements of this methodology, I was not inclined to pursue this

> *type of research myself. I was more interested in field*
> *research focusing on larger units of interaction.*

So, once Warner was gone and Chapple and Arensberg were cast out, the Harvard thrust was lost. Only Chapple seemed to understand the full implications of the earlier collective effort. A few years later he (Chapple, 1953, p. 304), put it succinctly, "We can, in fact, use a modified form of the kind of network analysis used in electrical work…and we can determine the effects of any change in the quantitative values assigned to any link on its neighbors in the network pattern."

I conclude, then, that although the work at Harvard contained all four of the features that define social network analysis, it failed to generate enough long-range commitment to be able to form, and to convince others that they had formed, a general paradigm for research. The group disintegrated because people—in particular, Warner—left and went on to other collaborations on other kinds of research. Moreover, another reason the Harvard group failed to form an identifiable paradigm for research probably stems from the fact that it developed internal conflicts. The other members of the Harvard group were apparently not ready to move off in the new direction proposed by Chapple and Arensberg: they were not prepared to embrace the rigor in procedures for data collection and the formal algebraic modeling suggested by Chapple and Arensberg. In fact, in the quotation above, Roethlisberger was troubled enough to describe the Chapple-Arensberg initiative as "a threat."

So the Harvard effort never "took off." It never provided a general model for a structural paradigm. As a matter of fact, the efforts at Harvard are almost never recognized in historical reviews of social network analysis.[22] Of the Harvard group, Homans is sometimes mentioned as an intellectual antecedent and the studies by Roethlisberger and Dickson and by Davis, Gardner and Gardner are sometimes credited with having generated early network data. But the organized collective work centered in the Business College and the Society of Fellows has

---

[22]The one exception I can find is in Scott's (2000) text

simply not been acknowledged as a central part of the history of the field.

Following Moreno's work and that at Harvard, social network analysis seemed to pass into a period that might be called "dark ages." Chapters 5, 6 and 7 deal with this period. For a span of thirty years, from about 1940 until about 1970, no major centers of social network research emerged. However, as we shall see in these three chapters, there were quite a number of small efforts that kept the structural perspective alive.

Chapter 5

Social Network Analysis During the Dark Ages I: the 1940s

By the 1940s, much of the excitement that Moreno and Jennings had generated in the 1930s had already started to wane. Moreover, the Harvard group had broken up and its members had drifted away from structural analysis. So the period in question was essentially a kind of "dark ages" for social network analysis. There was no generally recognized approach to social research that embodied the structural paradigm. Social network analysis was still not identifiable either as a theoretical perspective or as an approach to data collection and analysis.

That fact, however, did not mean that no social network research was done during the period in question. As we shall see, a number of people at a number of universities kept the structural perspective alive. None of these efforts, however, had enough impact to be widely adopted as a general paradigm for the structural approach.

Doubtless many of these people were influenced by the earlier work at Harvard or, even more likely, by the early popularity of the contributions by Moreno and Jennings. But at least some of these latter day network scholars more or less independently came up with the social network paradigm. In the next several sections I will review a series of settings in which investigators working in the 1940s produced research that was essentially network analytic.

5.1 A Mobile Group: From Iowa to MIT to Michigan in the 1930s and 1940s

Figure 5.1. Kurt Lewin (before he immigrated to America)

The next development in research that embodied the social network perspective was originated by a psychologist, Kurt Lewin.[23] Lewin, shown in Figure 5.1, was born in Germany in 1890. He received a PhD in experimental psychology from the University of Berlin in 1916. He served in the German army during World War I. After the war he accepted a position in the Psychological Institute of the Berlin University where he worked with the eminent Gestalt psychologists Max Wertheimer and Wolfgang Koehler. In 1933, like many German Jews of that era, he fled the Nazi regime and came to the United States.

Lewin's first job in America was in the Home Economics Department at Cornell. But, in 1935 he was hired by the Child Welfare Research Station at the University of Iowa. When he arrived at Iowa, Lewin's research was focused on what he called "field theory," or "topological psychology." It stressed the importance of internal and external "forces" as they might impinge on an individual's behavior. Thus, his approach considered the impact of situational factors in determining behavior (Lewin, 1936).

---

[23]He pronounced his name the German way, Leveen, with the accent on the second syllable.

Among the situational factors that Lewin took into account in understanding an individual's behavior, were the effects of the behaviors of other people (Patnoe, 1988, p. 5). Beginning at the time he moved to Iowa, however, he began to shift his interest from the study of individual behavior to the study of interpersonal relations and group processes.

Above all, Lewin was a gifted teacher. For him, research and teaching were wrapped together into a single integrated package. The way he worked was by talking to other people, his colleagues, his students—anyone and everyone. He made no status claims and this contributed to his attraction as a teacher. So, at Iowa, Lewin trained a whole generation of American social psychologists. All were imbued with a respect for empirical—particularly experimental—research. He was a charismatic figure, and because of that, he managed to attract a great many talented young psychologists as graduate and post-doctoral students. They included Alex Bavelas, Dorwin (Doc) Cartwright, Leon Festinger, John R. P. French, Jr., Ronald Lippett, Marian Radke and Alvin Zander.

In 1945 Lewin left Iowa to form the Research Center for Group Dynamics at MIT. He was joined by four of his former students, Dorwin Cartwright, Leon Festinger, Ronald Lippitt and Marian Radke. In addition, Lewin also brought along a fifth young man who was still a graduate student, Alex Bavelas.

The moment this group arrived at MIT they began to attract more students. The early recruits included Kurt Back, Morton Deutsch, Gordon Hearn, Harold Kelley, Albert Pepitone, Stanley Schachter and John Thibaut.

This was an immensely productive period for the Research Center for Group Dynamics. Patnoe (1988, p. 9) described just how productive it was:

> *During the three years they were in residence at MIT, research was designed and carried out on such issues as leadership (Lippitt & French, 1948), group cohesiveness (Back, 1951; Thibaut, 1950), group productivity (French, 1950), the effects of group membership on it's members (Schachter, 1951), cooperation and*

competition (Deutsch, 1949), intergroup relations (Lippitt & Radke, 1946), communication and the spread of influence within groups (Festinger, Schachter & Back, 1950; Festinger & Thibaut, 1951) and social perception (Kelley, 1950; Pepitone, 1950).

Amid all this productivity, disaster hit the program in 1947. Lewin died suddenly and unexpectedly. He was replaced by one of his former students, John (Jack) French, Jr.[24] But President Compton of MIT soon decided that, without Lewin, the Research Center was no more than an expensive frill in an engineering school, one that they could do without. So Cartwright and Festinger set out to find another home.

Before and during the war, Cartwright had worked with Rensis Likert, a sociologist at the University of Michigan. So, through Likert's intervention, the whole Research Center for Group Dynamics was invited to move to the University of Michigan. The move was made in 1948. Cartwright, Festinger, French and Lippitt took with them several graduate students, including Harold Kelley, Stanley Schachter and John Thibaut. And, before leaving, both Cartwright and Festinger helped Lewin's graduate student Alex Bavelas to finish his degree and get started on his own research.

Cartwright took over for Lewin and directed Bavelas' dissertation. Bavelas completed his PhD at MIT in 1948 and was immediately invited to join the faculty. He did, and he designed a landmark study of the implications of social network structure.

When he took the job at MIT, Bavelas (shown in Figure 5.2) was already armed with an important structural intuition (Bavelas, 1948). He believed that in any organization the degree to which a single individual dominates its communication network—the degree to which it was centralized—affected its efficiency, its morale and the perceived influence of each individual actor. Since the Research Center for Group Dynamics was leaving for Michigan, Bavelas created a new—presumably less ex-

---

[24]French had received his PhD from Harvard, but he too had been trained by Lewin during Lewin's visiting appointments at Harvard in 1938 and 1939.

pensive—center, the Group Networks Laboratory, as a part of MIT's established Lincoln Laboratory.

Festinger helped in the development of Bavelas' new lab by introducing him to R. Duncan Luce. Luce recalled the event (1978, p.247):

Figure 5.2. Alex Bavelas

> *The actual start of my career in psychology was, in a sense, sharply defined. One afternoon, Albert Perry, a graduate student in electrical engineering at MIT, and I were modifying a military surplus radio into what then passed for high-fidelity equipment, when my roommate William Blitzer returned from Leon Festinger's class in social psychology. He described to us some of the combinatorial problems they faced in dealing with social networks. Soon Perry and I were busy trying to translate these into questions about matrices, and a few days later Blitzer introduced us, with some theorems in hand, to Festinger. By the end of the summer we had a paper ready for submission, and another paper on the same topic followed shortly.*

The paper that was "ready for submission" was the classic paper—one of the most important in social network analysis—in which Luce and Perry (1949) formally defined the notion of "clique."

At that time Luce was working on his PhD in mathematics at MIT and was looking for a job. Festinger introduced Luce to Bavelas and Luce was hired as "Bavelas' captive mathematician" (Luce, 1978, p. 248). Bavelas put Luce to work, along with a collection of social science students. The job was to work out a way to study the consequences of communication structure. The crew included Bavelas and Luce, along with Robert P. Abelson, Harold Leavitt, Lois Rogge, Arnold Simmel and Sidney Smith. Under Bavelas' leadership, they developed a formal model, drew graph theoretic images of social structures, designed an experiment, and collected experimental data on efficiency, morale and the recognition of leadership. Their work indicated that Bavelas' original intuition had been correct in every respect (Bavelas, 1950; Leavitt, 1951; Smith, 1950).

The work of the MIT group, then, displayed all the elements that are found in contemporary social network analysis. It embodied a structural intuition. It involved the collection of systematic experimental data. It used the graphs shown in Figure 5.5 to represent the patterns of communication that were studied. And the Bavelas group developed a formal model for their main independent variable, centrality.

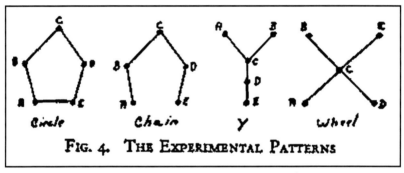

Figure 5.3. Experimental communication forms studied by the Bavelas group

At the time, Bavelas' research generated widespread interest. People from several fields, including Claude Flament (1956) from psychology, Harold Guetzkow (Guetzkow and Dill, 1957) from political science and the Nobel Laureate Herbert Simon (Guetzkow and Simon, 1955) from economics wrote follow-ups extending the Bavelas approach. But that interest quickly waned. Bavelas left MIT in 1950 to work on a State Department project and turned the research laboratory over to Lee S. Christie and Duncan Luce. Bavelas worked in industry for years and never returned to his experimental structural analyses. Luce and Simmel moved to Columbia. So the impetus at MIT dried up. Others did pick up parts of the MIT idea but very few really got the whole picture. As I summarized the problem (Freeman et al., 1980), "…subsequent investigators tended to be concerned either with conceptual problems of centrality or with the consequences of communication structure on problem solving, not both." This meant that the integration developed at MIT was lost. Each of the newer investigators focused on part of the total social network picture, but lost its generality.

The MIT part of the story, then, was over. But the same levels of energy and creativity were kept alive at Michigan. The structuralists at Michigan continued to be impressively productive. Their work maintained the Lewin style; it was usually experimental and it continued to involve both faculty and graduate students.

Once they were established at Michigan, Cartwright and Festinger both recognized a need for a mathematical collaborator—one who could help them explore the potential of "new mathematical techniques" in behavioral sciences. They received a grant from the Rockefeller Foundation, and Cartwright contacted the Chair of Michigan's Mathematics Department to seek a collaborator. The Chair thought the idea of mathematical social or behavioral science was crazy, but he did provide a name, Frank Harary, a new PhD teaching in the Department who had not yet chosen his area of specialization.

Since he had some mathematical training (and perhaps because he had provided the link between Bavelas and the mathematician, Luce, at MIT), Festinger made the first contact with Harary. They sat down together and Festinger drew the graph of the simple social structure shown in Figure 5.4. Harary reports that the moment he saw Festinger's graph his whole career appeared before him like a vision; he began a long and distinguished career focusing for the most part on applications of graph theory to problems of social structure (Hage and Harary, 1983; Harary, 1953, 1955; Harary and Norman, 1953; Harary and Ross, 1957).

At first Harary worked with Festinger, but when Festinger moved to Minnesota in 1951 and was no longer available, Harary and Cartwright teamed up. Their earliest major joint effort drew on the theory of signed graphs. They developed a formal state-

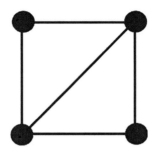

Figure 5.4. The Festinger graph[25]

ment of the notion of cognitive balance proposed by the psychologist Heider (Cartwright and Harary, 1956). And, from that start, a career-long collaboration was born.

Various subsets of the Michigan group worked on interpersonal influence and on rumor transmission (Back, 1951; Back, Festinger, Hymovitch, Kelley, Schachter and Thibaut, 1950; Festinger, Schachter and Back, 1950). In addition, in the mid 1950s Newcomb (1961) and Nordlie (1958) began collecting data for their path-breaking multi-year study of interpersonal attraction in a university residence hall.

There is a legitimate question, however, about the independence of all of this Lewin-inspired work from Moreno's sociometry. On several occasions in 1935 Moreno had met with Lewin and several of his students (Morrow, 1947). After those meetings, according to Moreno (1953, p. lxiv), Lewin exhibited a "…change in focus and attention from individual and Gestalt psychology to the consideration of group and action methods." Moreno argued, then, that the whole impetus for the MIT Research Center for Group Dynamics was built on his ideas.

Given Moreno's tendency toward paranoia, it would be easy to dismiss this argument as a paranoid fantasy. Renshaw (1981), for example, argues that Lewin did shift focus, but that his shift was the result of his association with established research practices at the University of Iowa's Child Welfare Institute:

---

[25]Harary wears a picture of this graph on his cap to this day.

> *Lewin's innovative research on group climates (Lewin, Lippit and White, 1939) was foreshadowed at Iowa in the research by Jack (1934), Page (1936), and H. Anderson (1937) on children's style of interaction....Thus, while Lewin's contribution should be acknowledged as a new and creative one, it appears that his going to Iowa in 1936 and reading the research already completed there on styles of peer interaction was a significant influence on the development of his ideas.*

In addition, Patnoe (1988, p. 31) quotes Cartwright about how Lippit, one of Lewin's early students at Iowa, influenced his mentor's thinking:

> *This impact of Lippitt's cannot be overemphasized. His role was very important. Lippitt had a tremendous influence on Lewin to get him interested in groups specifically.*

On the other hand, Wech (1996), who is a Lewin supporter, made a careful examination of all the relevant data. Her conclusion was that the meetings with Moreno did affect Lewin's work. And Lewin, moreover, was an early publisher in Moreno's journal (Lewin and Lippitt, 1938).

We end up, then, with no sure answer. Lewin's perspective did change direction when he went to Iowa. But whether that was due to the influence of researchers already working at Iowa or the result of the influence of Moreno is not clear.

To my mind, the question of influence here is beside the point. The Iowa-MIT-Michigan group went far beyond the sociometry of Moreno. The two research traditions shared the intuitive notion that people's social ties to others have important consequences for their lives. But beyond that intuitive foundation, the two went off in different directions. Moreno's work was based primarily on subjective responses to questionnaires. Lewin and his students manipulated social ties and collected experimental data about their consequences. And while mathematics was peripheral to most of Moreno's research, mathematics was at the core of the work at MIT and Michigan. Finally, while both projects used graphics, Bavelas, Luce, Festinger, Cartwright and Harary used them explicitly in the context of the formalisms of graph theory. The differences, I think, are large enough to suggest that Lewin's research—and particularly that of his students—was a good deal more than simply derivative.

All in all, the Iowa-MIT-Michigan years were a highly productive period for an impressive collection of research scientists. They worked on a wide range of structural problems and collected an immense amount of systematic relational data. They used graph theoretic images regularly. They developed formal models. And it is clear from their easy transition from application to application that they recognized the generality of their social network approach. This recognition was explicitly made years later in the publication *Structural Models: An Introduction to the Theory of Directed Graphs* (Harary, Norman and Cartwright, 1965). That book set out a generalized abstract representation of social networks in precise terms.

Thus, the Iowa-MIT-Michigan axis succeeded in producing a huge amount of important theory and data over an extended period. Their structural approach was generalized to a wide range of empirical phenomena. It had a profound impact on research in social psychology. Moreover, in retrospect, their work is generally recognized as an important influence in the genesis of contemporary social network research.

In a very muddled statement, Mullins and Mullins (1973) characterized this Lewin-led effort as completely unrelated to the study of social networks. They defined the Lewineans as focused exclusively on the study of small groups, and they listed a rag-tag collection of any others who had ever talked about small groups as members of Lewin's "theory group." The list included, for example, Elliot Chapple, George Homans and William Foote Whyte, as well as Jacob Moreno and Helen Jennings, among the members of the Lewin group.[26] Chapple, Homans and Whyte were, as we saw, associated with Warner, not Lewin,

---

[26]Most remarkably, they consistently referred to Jacob Moreno as "José Moreno."

and Moreno and Jennings were at the core of the sociometric approach. At the same time, the Mullins and Mullins list did not include Harrison White or any of his students. So, in effect, they grouped Warner's people, Moreno's people and Lewin's people together into a single clump, but they saw no similarities between the research efforts of any of these people and the structural approach of Harrison White.[27]

In any case, Mullins and Mullins concluded that the Lewin team had failed. According to their analysis, it failed because after Lewin's death, it lacked both intellectual and organizational leadership and was unable to attract students. But when we consider the major intellectual and organizational contributions of Bavelas, Cartwright, Festinger and Newcomb, this argument falls apart. As a freshman faculty member at MIT, Bavelas designed a breakthrough experiment, organized a new research laboratory and recruited students like Robert P. Abelson, Harold Leavitt and Arnold Simmel, all of whom went on to stellar careers. Cartwright organized the movement of Lewin's laboratory from MIT to Michigan and went on to be one of the authors of a book that is still the most authoritative text on the application of graph theory to social network analysis (Harary, Norman and Cartwright, 1965). Festinger is often described as "the father of experimental social psychology" (Patnoe, p. 255), and Newcomb (1961) conducted a study of the acquaintanceship process that is still cited by people working in social network analysis more than forty years later. This group, moreover, trained a whole generation of productive social psychologists, including such notables as Elliot Aronson, Kurt W. Back, Judson Mills, Stanley Schachter and John W. Thibaut.

The Lewinean perspective came to dominate the field of social psychology, and the people involved are still cited regularly by network analysts. But it failed to be picked up as a general paradigm for other social research disciplines of the time.

---

[27]Nicholas C. Mullins was one of White's social network students.

5.2 Michigan State College in the mid 1940s

In Chapter 3, I suggested that most of Moreno's early supporters quickly drifted away. But a few did keep the sociometric faith. Notable among these was a rural sociologist, Charles P. Loomis. Loomis had grown up in a farming family in Las Cruces, New Mexico. After he received a bachelor's degree in 1928 from the New Mexico College of Agriculture and Mechanical Arts, he went on for a master's at North Carolina State College. Then, as a contemporary of Warner's students, Loomis went to Harvard for his PhD and received a degree in sociology in 1933. Loomis was in graduate school, then, during the time when Warner was introducing the structural perspective at Harvard.

There is no evidence, however, that Loomis had any significant contact with Warner or his colleagues and students at that time. Warner's efforts were concentrated in the Business School and the Anthropology Department and Loomis apparently worked entirely in the Sociology and Economics Departments. In particular, he worked with the Chairman of Sociology, Pitirim Sorokin, who, as we saw in Chapter 3, had very little to do with the structuralists centered in the Business School. Loomis's doctoral thesis, moreover, was a fairly standard demographic study of North Carolina farmers.

After receiving his degree, Loomis was hired into a research position at the United States Department of Agriculture. There he began using sociometric tools to do research in rural communities (Loomis and Davidson, 1939). Then, in 1944, he accepted a position as Head of the Sociology and Anthropology Department at Michigan State College.

At Michigan State, Loomis trained a large number of graduate students in the use of sociometric research tools (Driscoll et al., 1993). With their help, he conducted a series of comparative studies of small villages and rural areas throughout the world. (Examples are Loomis, 1946; Holland and Loomis, 1948; Loomis and Powell, 1949; Loomis and Proctor, 1950.)[28]

---

[28]The Holland cited here was the father of the prominent social network statistician, Paul W. Holland. John B. Holland received his PhD at Michigan State with Loomis, then took his family and went to work on a Loomis project in Cuba where he died of a sudden and unexpected heart attack.

At the same time, Loomis recognized the importance of mathematics in structural research and sought out colleagues in mathematics to help him deal with the complexities of network analysis. Prominent among those was the mathematical statistician Leo Katz, who had received his PhD from the University of Michigan in 1945. Reportedly, Loomis showed Katz some of the statistical work in sociometry and Katz was intrigued, because until then, the field had developed only very primitive models. According to Katz's student Charles Proctor,[29] "Katz jumped at the chance to clean things up and to advance them." Proctor went on to add that, as a recent PhD from the University of Michigan, Katz was motivated further by a spirit of "…competition with theorists at U of M…such as Leon Festinger and Frank Harary."

Over the next few years, then, Katz produced a series of papers that made major contributions to sociometry and, in the long run, to social network analysis (Forsyth and Katz, 1946; Katz, 1947; Katz and Powell, 1955; Bhargava and Katz, 1963). In addition Katz led several students in mathematics to work on applied problems in structural analysis. Among these, Charles Proctor and T. N. Bhargava made important contributions.

Thus, the Loomis/Katz group at Michigan State helped keep sociometry alive. And they contributed to the development of social network analysis in two ways. Led by Loomis, they conducted high quality research on rural areas and small villages. Those studies are still cited by network analysts. And, led by Katz, they developed an important collection of new probability-based formal models. These projects both extended the sociometric approach, but apparently their efforts were not enough to re-kindle widespread interest in sociometry.

5.3 The University of Chicago and the Sorbonne in the late 1940s

Another early effort that involved a structural perspective also emerged in the 1940s. It was generated by Claude Lévi-

---

[29]Personal communication.

Strauss and drew on the mathematical skills of André Weil.[30] Lévi-Strauss is shown in Figure 5.5.

Figure 5.5. Claude Lévi-Strauss

Lévi-Strauss was born in 1908 in Belgium to French parents. His family returned to France when he was a year old and so he grew up in Paris. He was an outstanding student and was admitted to the *École Normale Superieure* that was, as its name implies, a very good university. Lévi-Strauss first studied law, then switched and received his degree in philosophy. His fellow students included Simone Weil and Jean-Paul Sartre, both of whom later became famous philosophers.

After receiving his degree Lévi-Strauss got a job teaching philosophy. In 1933 he began reading ethnography and in it found his natural intellectual home. So in 1935, he accepted a professorship at the University of São Paulo in Brazil. His presence in South America permitted him to follow his interest in ethnography by doing fieldwork among the Caduveo and Bororo Indian tribes of the Amazon basin.

---

[30]He pronounced his name "Vay" in the French manner.

He returned to France in 1939, but the war drove him out again. In 1941 he took a job teaching at the New School for Social Research in New York. While he was teaching at the New School, Lévi-Strauss was trying to make sense of the wide range of differing kinship patterns. The rules of who was considered to be related to whom and who could marry whom in various societies seemed, at first, to be arbitrary. But then one of his colleagues, a linguist named Roman Jakobson, introduced him to the work of Ferdinand de Saussure. Saussure et al. (1916) had studied the structure of languages. He proposed that though the rules of grammar vary from language to language, the words are always related to each other according to *some* system of rules.

Lévi-Strauss thereafter set out to uncover the systems of rules that various peoples used to determine kinship. When the war was over, he returned to France and in 1948 defended his PhD dissertation at the University of Paris. In his dissertation he took a structural approach to the study of kinship. A year later he turned that dissertation into a major book, *Les Structures élémentaires de la Parenté* [The Elementary Structures of Kinship] (1949/1969). In that book, Lévi-Strauss examined "…preferential marriage based on definite kinship relations." (Josselin de Jong, 1970, p. 2). He concluded that all preferential marriages are based on some form of exchange (Lévi-Strauss, 1949/1969, pp. 478–479). Such exchange creates alliances (Hénaff, 1998, p. 89). And alliances are essential to ensure "…the integration of partial units within the total group." (Lévi-Strauss, 1949/1969, p. 481). They are "the only way of maintaining the group as a group…" (Lévi-Strauss, 1949/1969, p. 479).

It is clear, then, that Lévi-Strauss took a general structural approach to the study of kinship and marriage. More than that, he based his conclusions on his analysis of dozens of data sets from societies throughout the world. He used visual images consistently, including genealogical charts and directed graphs like the one shown in Figure 5.6. And he prevailed on André Weil to produce an algebraic appendix for his book.

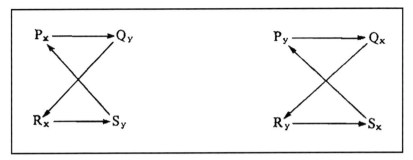

Figure 5.6. Directed graphs from Lévi-Strauss

André Weil was the brother of the philosopher, Simone Weil, who had attended school with Lévi-Strauss. Weil was born in Paris in 1906. He had always been intrigued by mathematics, and he received his Ph.D. in that subject in 1928 from the University of Paris. He taught at various foreign universities, but finally he obtained a regular appointment at the University of Strasbourg in France in 1933. There, he was the principal force behind the publications of Nicholas Bourbaki. An economist, Steven E. Landsburg (http://www.netacc.net/~fairplay/weil.htm), described how this happened:

> *In 1934, Bourbaki sprang full-blown from the head of Andre Weil. Weil was teaching at Strasbourg and engaged in endless discussions with his colleague Henri Cartan about the "right" way to present various mathematical concepts to students. It occurred to him these discussions were probably being duplicated by his friends in other universities all over France. Weil proposed that they all meet to settle these questions once and for all. "Little did I know," wrote Weil, "that at that moment Bourbaki was born."*

Bourbaki, then, was a pseudonym used by a collection of young French mathematicians. They worked together, and together made a series of major contributions to the foundations of mathematics.

In 1947 Weil accepted an appointment at the University of Chicago, where he remained until 1958. At that point he left

Chicago, bound for Princeton, New Jersey, where he joined the faculty of the Institute for Advanced Study. Throughout his career he continued to make major contributions to mathematics. Arguably, Weil was *the* French mathematician of his generation.

Lévi-Strauss provided both the intuitive background and the data for Weil's algebraic modeling. Weil, in turn, developed a model for one of the most complicated kinship systems, the Australian Murngin, who had been studied by W. Lloyd Warner. Lévi-Strauss described his basis for asking Weil to build a model (1960):

> *I fail to see why an algebraic treatment of, let us say, symbols for marriage rules, could not teach us, when aptly manipulated, something about the way a given marriage system actually works, and bring out properties not immediately apparent at the empirical level.*

Both Lévi-Strauss and Weil used graphic images in their treatment of kinship. Jointly they produced a work that included all of the properties of social network analysis. Although they did draw on the earlier work of Radcliff-Brown, there is no reason to believe that they were even aware of Moreno's work or the efforts of the Harvard group. My guess is that theirs was largely an independent development of a social network perspective.

Despite the fact that Lévi-Strauss and Weil provided a general model for social network analysis, it never seemed to capture the imagination of people working in other areas of social research. Subsequent follow-ups (Kemeny, Snell and Thompson, 1957; White, 1963; Courrège, 1965; Boyd, 1969; Ballonoff, 1974) all extended and refined the Lévi-Strauss-Weil models, but their extensions were confined to the analysis of kinship data. Lévi-Strauss himself went on to study mythology, and dropped his interest in social behavior.

Chapter 6

Social Network Analysis During the Dark Ages II: the 1950s

6.1 Lund University in the early 1950s

Early in the 1950s an effort was started at Lund University in Sweden. It was led by a Swedish geographer, Torsten Hägerstrand. Hägerstrand grew up living above his schoolteacher father's schoolhouse in a rural area called Småland. He entered the University of Lund in 1937 where he studied both geography and art history. In 1938 he was appointed as a librarian and teaching assistant, but he gradually drifted into geography as a full-time study.

Hägerstrand and his future wife decided to trace the lives of every person who had lived in the Swedish rural area of Asby from 1840 to 1940. All in all, they recorded the lives and migration patterns of more than 10,000 people.

But Hägerstrand was uncomfortable with the purely descriptive, archival approach of most geographers of the time. He read widely in other fields and was particularly impressed by the astrophysicist, Sir Arthur Eddington; the sociologist, George Lundberg and the mathematician-biologist, A. J. Lotka. He also read and was influenced by the works of Jacob Moreno and Kurt Lewin. So he set out to do theory-based structural work in geography.

His theory-based research got started when his old friend, the Swedish mathematician/computer scientist Carl-Erik Fröberg, returned from a year of work in the U.S. In his travels Fröberg had discovered that some American mathematicians were working with random numbers. He returned to Sweden with a small pamphlet that described a 1949 symposium on the Monte Carlo Method. Fröberg presented this idea in a colloquium at Lund, and reportedly, most of his colleagues ridiculed it. But the presentation did capture Hägerstrand's imagination and he set out to do a computer simulation of the spread of innovations across space and time.

By means of a time-dated sequence of maps, Hägerstrand was able to show that innovations spread from their points of origin in a wave-like pattern. His research objective, then, was to identify the process underlying that pattern. He guessed that a process of pair-wise communication—from adopter to adopter—could account for the kind of patterning he had observed. So he set himself the task of building a computer model to determine whether those patterns could be produced by that kind of person-to-person diffusion process. His plan was to use random numbers to develop a Monte Carlo simulation of his assumed pair-wise diffusion process. Interestingly enough, Lund did not yet have a computer, so in his first attempts he had to emulate a computer simulation using only a desk calculator.

Hägerstrand assumed that a person was more likely to pass information to another who was geographically close than to one who was distant. But he needed a way to estimate the likelihood of contact at various distances. To do that, he used existing data on the distances between the addresses of pairs of people who married in the region he was studying. The marriage data did show that there was a decrease in the probability of marriage with increasing geographic distance between the addresses of the bride and groom. He used these marriage figures to estimate the probabilities of interpersonal contacts at various distances. In addition, he used demographic data on the distribution of the population to specify the number of potential targets for diffusion at each location in the region he was studying.

His simulation began by specifying an innovation along with a map of some region for which he had sequential data on the spread of that innovation through space. He located the actual point of origin and used that to begin his simulation of spatial diffusion. The simulation embodied a discrete time process—a series of cycles. At each cycle, each established adopter passed the innovation on to one new target person. The target was randomly chosen, but choices were biased by the distance-decay statistics produced from the marriage data. The simulation, then, generated a sequence of maps of the spread of an innovation through space and over time. And the maps produced by simulation showed the same wave-like patterning displayed by the empirical maps (Hägerstrand, 1952).

Clearly, this work was motivated by an important structural intuition—the pair-wise passage of information through a population. Hägerstrand created images of the actual and the simulated spread of various innovations. They were so similar that his computer simulation of a computational model lent credence to his pair-wise diffusion hypothesis.

Hägerstrand's work was structural. It displayed all the features of social network analysis. He provided a model for a geography that explored theoretical issues and attempted to explain the distributions of objects in physical space. That approach had a tremendous impact on the field of geography and led a whole generation of geographers to do similar kinds of structural work. They include Brian J. L. Berry (Garrison, Berry, Marble, Morrill and Nystuen, 1959; Berry, 1964), Lawrence A. Brown (1981), Michael Dacey (1964), William Garrison (1960), Peter R. Gould (Gould and White, 1974), Duane F. Marble (Garrison, Berry, Marble, Morrill and Nystuen, 1959), Richard Morrill (Garrison, Berry, Marble, Morrill and Nystuen, 1959), Forrest R. Pitts (1965, 1979) and Waldo R. Tobler (1965). Unfortunately, the impact of Hägerstrand's structural research was pretty much confined to the field of geography. Apparently, the links between social geographers and other social scientists were too weak to encourage adoption of this approach as a general model for structural research.

6.2 The University of Chicago in the early 1950s

Another center of structural studies was established at the University of Chicago in the 1950s. At that time, Nicolas Rashevsky was the Chair of the Committee on Mathematical Biology at Chicago. Rashevsky was born in Russia in 1899 and educated as a mathematical physicist. He came to the United States in 1924 and began working at the Westinghouse Electric and Manufacturing Company and teaching as an Instructor in Physics at the University of Pittsburgh. While teaching at Pittsburgh, he came up with the radical notion of building a field of mathematical biophysics patterned after mathematical physics.

Meanwhile, in 1929, at the age of 30, Robert Maynard Hutchins left the Yale Law School to become President of the University of Chicago. Hutchins was an innovator who objected to the rigidity and specialization he saw in higher education. As a college president, then, he sought out innovative academic programs. Thus, Hutchins hired Rashevsky in 1935.

Chicago's flexibility under Hutchins made it easy for Rashevsky to develop a Committee on Mathematical Biophysics (later renamed the Committee on Mathematical Biology). The Committee—essentially only Rashevsky at the beginning—developed a doctoral program that drew support from the Rockefeller Foundation. Rashevsky regularly taught a seminar that was attended by both faculty and students. He founded a journal, the *Bulletin of Mathematical Biophysics*. And, from the beginning he succeeded in attracting notable associates.

Perhaps the most noteworthy of Rashevsky's early students was Walter Pitts, who is generally recognized as the founder of neural net modeling. Writing in the Encyclopedia of the Cognitive Sciences at MIT, Lettvin (n.d.) described Pitts as follows:

> *Pitts appeared as a penniless 14-year-old at the University of Chicago in 1937, attended various classes, though unregistered, and was accepted by Rashevsky's coterie as a very talented but mysterious junior. All that was known of him was that he came from Detroit, and that would be all that was known thereafter....In 1938 he appeared at the office of Ru-*

*dolf Carnap, whose most recent book on logic had ap-
peared the previous year. Without introducing himself, Pitts laid out his copy opened to a section
annotated marginally, and proceeded to make critical
comments on the material. Carnap, after initial shock,
defended his work and engaged with Pitts in an hour
or so of talk. Pitts then left with his copy. For several
weeks, Carnap hunted through the university for "that
newsboy who understood logic," finally located him,
and found a job for him, for Pitts had no funds and
lived only on what he could earn from ghosting papers for other students.*

A great deal of the early work of the Committee was focused on modeling neural connections, but by the 1950s most of
Rashevsky's own work had shifted to applications of mathematics to sociological issues. This focus emerged because he (Rashevsky, 1949) believed that:

*…a logical extension of the mathematical biology of
behavior leads into mathematical sociology. The envi-
ronmental parameters, which determine some of our
reactions, are themselves determined by the reactions
of other individuals. Thus we are led from the "problem of one individual" to the more general "problem
of n individuals," and thence into the domain of the
social sciences.*

At that time, the faculty in Rashevsky's Committee included Herbert D. Landahl, Alfonso Shimbel, Hyman G. Landau and
Anatol Rapoport. And their students included Ray J. Solomonoff
and Lionel I. Rebhun. Solomonoff went on to a distinguished
career in algorithmic probability, and Rebhun became a prominent biologist. Figure 6.1 shows the attendance at a session of
Rashevsky's seminar in 1951.

Both the faculty and the students followed Rashevsky's lead
and developed models of social behavior. In the early 1950s Rapoport (Rapoport, 1953, 1954, 1957; Rapoport and Rebhun, 1952;
Solomonoff and Rapoport, 1951) followed up Rashevsky's (1951a,
1951b) work on the interpersonal process underlying the diffu-

Figure 6.1. The Rashevsky seminar (Rashevsky is seated in the front row nearest the camera. Rapoport is next, followed by Shimbel and Landau. The lecturer is Landahl).

sion of information. Solomonoff and Rapoport (1951), Landau (1952), Landau and Rapoport (1953) and Landahl (1953a, 1953b) all reported work on the same problem. At the same time, first Rapoport (1949a, 1949b) and then Landau (1951a, 1951b, 1953) worked on developing formal models of dominance hierarchies. Landau's efforts were so successful that his 1953 paper is still cited regularly by mathematicians who work in the area of "score sequences."

Rapoport was a key participant in all of this work. He was born in Russia in 1911. He came to the United States in 1922 and became a naturalized citizen in 1928. After high school, he spent two years as a student of piano in Chicago. Then, in 1929, he went to Europe and studied at the State Academy of Music in Vienna. He became a concert pianist and from 1933 through 1937 he appeared regularly on the concert stage in Europe, the United States and Mexico.

He then returned to school as a student at the University of Chicago. Because he had heard that musical talent and mathematical aptitude were highly correlated, he chose to study mathematics. As part of that pursuit he introduced himself to

Rashevsky and began to sit in on his seminars. In any case, his studies went well and he received his PhD in mathematics on December 5, 1941. After the Pearl Harbor attack two days later, Rapoport immediately joined the U. S. Air Corps and served as an officer during World War II. After the war he got a job teaching mathematics at the Illinois Institute of Technology, but Rashevsky soon hired him to teach mathematics and biology at the University of Chicago.

Landau and Landahl were also major contributors. Landahl was born in the United States and graduated from St. Olaf College in Northfield, Minnesota, in 1934. He was awarded a PhD in Mathematics at the University of Chicago in 1941 and he joined the Committee on Mathematical Biology as a faculty member in 1942. Landau was born in Poland in 1909 and came to the United States as a child. He was trained as a mathematician, first at Carnegie Tech and finally at the University of Pittsburgh where he received his PhD in 1946. He interrupted his studies during the war, and worked for the government on problems of ballistics. After the war he received his PhD and was hired by Rashevsky.

The members of the Committee—both faculty and students—were all essentially applied mathematicians. They focused almost exclusively on structural phenomena and speculated about the processes that might generate them. They produced both mathematical and computational models dealing with the patterning of links connecting humans or other animals. And although their use of graphic images was rare, they were sensitive to their importance. In discussing a dominance matrix, Landau (1951a), for example, said, "a geometric (topological) description of the structure can also be given by n points with lines connecting every pair of these points and a direction assigned to every line." Thus, he described a directed graph.

As mathematicians, then, members of the Committee focused on constructing models of social structure. And they certainly were aware of the generality of their structural models. Rashevsky (1968) made that point clear:

> ...history may be considered as the result of interactions between individuals...what a certain person

wrote, said, or did is largely, perhaps even completely, determined by the effects on his life produced by his fellow men…

But in addition to their mathematical modeling, these Committee members regularly drew on a variety of data sets. In one article, for example, Landau discussed his model in terms of Warder Clyde Allee's (1938) data on hens. And in the next, he talked about the same model in the light of Ruth Benedict's (1934) data on the Zuñi.

So it is clear that Rashevsky, Rapoport, Landau, Landahl and the rest of the Chicago mathematical biologists developed a generalized social network perspective. And given the fact that they were applied mathematicians, it is also likely that their work was largely independent of the work of Moreno and the other earlier social scientists.

Unfortunately, the whole effort at Chicago dried up just as it was getting established. Rapoport (2000, p. 106) described what happened:

> *Financial support for the University of Chicago (suspected of harbouring subversion) was drying up. To revive it, some assurance of loyalty to "American values" had to be shown. That meant that Hutchins had to go. A skilled money raiser unstained by either "intellectual elitism" or softness on Communism replaced him. The U.S. senatorial Jenner Committee (one of the committees investigating "un-American activities" on campuses) was welcomed at the University of Chicago.*
>
> *A group formed including people who were likely to be called to the hearings.…I was not called. Three of my colleagues, members of the Committee on Mathematical Biology, were called…Another colleague, (Landau) who had done research in ballistics during the war was asked whether he was engaged in espionage at that time. He turned to an attorney and asked him whether if he answered that question in the negative, he would be obliged to answer other questions.*

> *The attorney said he would. Then my colleague in-*
> *voked the Fifth Amendment and was excused from*
> *further testimony. He was fired. So was a third mem-*
> *ber of the Committee on Mathematical Biology. It was*
> *done delicately. Their contracts were simply not re-*
> *newed. I never found out why I was not called.*

In any case, with the departure of Hutchins, the University of Chicago became an inhospitable home for many of its faculty. Landau went to work in Mechanical Engineering at Columbia. And Rapoport moved to Palo Alto, California, for a year to become a fellow at the Center for Advanced Study in the Behavioral Sciences. During his year there, his closest contacts included Alex Bavelas and Duncan Luce (Rapoport, 2000, p. 112), both of whom had been part of the earlier MIT efforts.

Meanwhile, a general exodus from Chicago was planned. The psychologist, James G. Miller, led a group of faculty who moved from Chicago to the University of Michigan. They included David Easton, Ralph Gerard and Anatol Rapoport.[31] So with both Landau and Rapoport involved in other pursuits, the Committee on Mathematical Biology was gutted. It never revived its thrust toward structural modeling of social phenomena. Moreover, because of its name and almost certainly because of its mathematical bent, it never captured the attention of most social scientists. So again we see an effort that failed to open the social network approach to the larger world of social scientists.

6.3 Columbia University in the mid 1950s

In the mid 1950s, a collection of sociologists at Columbia University developed a general social network conception. The leaders of this effort were the lifelong collaborators Paul Lazarsfeld and Robert K. Merton. They are pictured in Figures 6.2 and 6.3.

Lazarsfeld and Merton were unlikely collaborators. As Merton (1998) put it, they were an "odd couple." Their social and intellectual backgrounds were completely different and their

---

[31] And one of my own graduate school mentors, Donald T. Campbell, left the Psychology Department at Chicago for Northwestern at the same time.

Figure 6.2. Paul Lazarsfeld

Figure 6.3. Robert Merton

styles of work were almost polar opposites. They were, in fact, hired by Columbia primarily because of their differences.

Merton (1998) described something of the background of the Columbia department:

> *Rather than being a matter of design, Paul's and my collaboration was a wholly unanticipated and delayed consequence of a deep division in the Columbia Department of Sociology that emerged in the late 1930s and early 1940s. The senior professors—Robert M. MacIver, the political and social theorist, and Robert S. Lynd, co-author of the famous* Middletown *series—had been at odds, both intellectually and personally, for years. As a result, they could not agree on any new senior appointment, and brought the department to a virtual standstill.*

Lazarsfeld (1975) described how he and Merton came to be hired into that context:

> *I had been director of a Rockefeller Foundation project to study the social effects of radio. Originally, the headquarters were in Princeton; but in 1939 the funds were transferred to Columbia, where I had been given the nominal title of lecturer, without faculty status. A year later, a full professorship in sociology became vacant, but the department could not agree on a nomination. The issue was whether the appointment should go to someone who emphasized social theory or to someone primarily concerned with empirical research. Finally, the professorial line was divided into two lower faculty positions, which were filled, respectively, by Merton and by me.*

So Columbia simultaneously hired these two young sociologists who were about as different as possible. They came from different continents, different social strata and different educational backgrounds. Moreover, they had different interests and they approached social research with vastly different styles.

Paul Lazarsfeld was born to intellectual, politically liberal, middle class parents in Vienna in 1901. His father was an attorney and his mother was a psychologist. Lazarsfeld attended the University of Vienna and received a PhD in mathematics in 1925. But his real interest was in psychology. So, after receiving his PhD, he took a part-time job working with Charlotte and Karl Bühler who had just founded a new department of psychology at the university.

Working in Vienna, Lazarsfeld began studies of both consumer behavior and the impact of unemployment. This work came to the attention of the Rockefeller Foundation, and they awarded him a fellowship in 1933 to visit the U.S. Once here, the political chaos in Austria convinced him to stay. He continued to work on developing what later came to be known as market research. This early work focused particularly on examining the impact of radio broadcasting on people's behavior.

Merton, in contrast, was born in a south Philadelphia slum in 1910. His birth name was Meyer R. Schkolnik. He grew up above his father's dairy products store. As a teenager, young Schkolnik began a career as a stage magician. With the hope of enhancing that career, he made up a stage name, "Robert King Merton." The name stuck and he used it after high school when he enrolled at Temple.

Calhoun (2003) described Merton's college career:

> *At Temple—a school founded for "the poor boys and girls of Philadelphia" and not yet fully accredited or matured into a university, he chanced on a wonderful undergraduate teacher. It was serendipity, the mature Merton insisted. The sociologist George E. Simpson took him on as a research assistant in a project on race and the media and introduced him not only to sociology but to Ralph Bunche and Franklin Frazier. Simpson also took Merton to the ASA annual meeting where he met Pitirim Sorokin, founding chair of the Harvard sociology department. He applied to Harvard, even though his teachers told him this was usually beyond the reach of those graduating from Temple. And*

> *when he arrived, Sorokin took him on as a research*
> *assistant. By Merton's second year they were pub-*
> *lishing together.*

Merton, then, was trained by Sorokin to be a theorist; he did not share Lazarsfeld's background in mathematics nor his commitment to methodology.

Thus Merton's background was the polar opposite of that of Lazarsfeld. Merton grew up in the U.S. in a working class family and was trained as a sociological theorist. Lazarsfeld came from a sophisticated Viennese middle-class upbringing. He was trained as a mathematician and he worked primarily as a sociological methodologist.[32] As Merton (1998) put it:

> ...we had been working in wholly disparate fields
> and had not even published in the same jour-
> nals....we also drew on entirely different tradi-
> tions of social and psychological thought.

According to Merton, when he and Lazarsfeld met, only 1.3% of their citations were to the same authors.

In the early 1940s, when he first came to Columbia as part of the radio research project, Lazarsfeld immediately began working with his new colleagues, Bernard Berelson, Hazel Gaudet and William McPhee. Together they launched a major study of voting behavior. Jerábek (2001) described that project:

> *...the researchers formulated the hypothesis of the* two-
> step flow of communication, *which argued against*
> *the idea of a universal direct effect of the mass media*
> *on everybody...[and they] also defined and identified*
> opinion leaders — *the people who take an interest in*
> *public goings-on and in information from the print,*
> *radio, and other mass media, and who then mediate*
> *the opinions and attitudes of the people around them*
> *(their followers).*

Since both of these ideas called attention to communications linking individuals, they both embody a structural perspective. They

---

[32]Some Columbia students of the period have suggested that, in the long run, Merton was the better methodologist and Lazarsfeld the better theorist.

show that Lazarsfeld and his colleagues at Columbia were already thinking in structural terms in the early 1940s (Lazarsfeld, Berelson and Gaudet, 1944; Lazarsfeld, Berelson and McPhee, 1953).

When Merton first joined the Columbia department and Lazarsfeld was officially appointed, they had virtually no contact. But fairly soon that changed. A *New Yorker* writer, Morton M. Hunt, wrote a piece in 1961 that described their initial contact (quoted in Lazarsfeld, 1975):

> *In November of 1941, Lazarsfeld felt that, as the older man, he ought to do the graceful thing and acknowledge the existence of his opposite number. He invited Merton to dinner, but on the afternoon of the engagement he got an urgent call from the Office of Facts and Figures (the predecessor of the O.W.I.),[33] requesting him to conduct an audience-reaction test that evening on a new radio program that had been devised as part of the agency's pre-war morale-building effort. When the Mertons arrived, Lazarsfeld met them at the door of his apartment and said, as the guests recall it, "How nice, how nice that you are here at last. But don't take off your coat, my dear Merton. I have a sociological surprise for you. We will leave the ladies to dine alone together, and we will return as soon as we can." Then he bustled Merton off to a radio studio where a score of people were listening to a recorded broadcast of "This Is War"....After the program, when an assistant of Lazarsfeld's questioned the audience on the reasons for its recorded likes and dislikes, Merton perked up; he detected theoretical shortcomings in the way the questions were being put. He started passing scribbled notes to Lazarsfeld....As a second batch of listeners entered the studio, Lazarsfeld asked Merton if he would do the post-program questioning.*

---

[33]Office of War Information, the government propaganda agency.

That was the beginning of the Lazarsfeld-Merton collaboration. As Calhoun (2003) put it, "Merton and Lazarsfeld formed an enormously productive partnership, training generations of students and developing a program of theoretically informed but empirically rigorous research."

That training included the education of a good many graduate students, but, as Calhoun (2003) described it, it went much farther:

> As important as each was as an individual intellectual, both Merton and Lazarsfeld may have been even more important as mentors and animators of an intellectual community at Columbia—and indeed beyond, at the Social Science Research Council, the Center for Advanced Study in the Behavioral Sciences, and the Russell Sage Foundation.

In general both Lazarsfeld and Merton influenced their students and colleagues to think in structural terms. In a personal communication, Charles Kadushin, who was a Columbia graduate student at the time, described the process:

> ...it was Merton who had us read Simmel (Georg, not Arnold who was in that seminar!) line by line. Simmel of course had nascent network ideas and it was the combination of Lazarsfeld's interest in personal influence and Merton's interest in Simmel that lead me to combine the two into a network theory of social circles.

Together Lazarsfeld and Merton worked on a range of projects. They produced an article on communication as early as 1948 (Lazarsfeld and Merton, 1948). And they wrote a major article on the formation of friendships six years later (Lazarsfeld and Merton, 1954). But perhaps their biggest contribution was in producing students who were prepared to develop projects on the cutting edge of social network research. First Menzel and Katz (1956), then Coleman, Katz and Menzel (1957) examined interpersonal factors in their classic study of the diffusion of drug information among physicians. Peter Blau (1977) developed the notion of homophily in which he argued that interaction is more likely among individuals with similar characteristics.[34] Charles Kadushin (1966) extended and specified Simmel's concept of "social circles." All of these Columbia students continued to work in a structuralist mode, and many of them produced another generation of students who themselves became major contributors.[35]

So the Columbia Department of Sociology and the Bureau of Applied Social Research became centers of structural thought. Their research was based on network data. Graphic images— particularly those based on matrix permutations—were used (Coleman and MacRae, 1960). And most of their work was designed to produce mathematical models. That the Columbia group recognized the generality of their network approach is demonstrated in the following final word included by Coleman, Katz and Menzel (1957):

> *A word should be added about the significance of re-search of this kind, aside from the possible interest in its specific substantive findings. It exemplifies a meth-odological approach which will, we feel, assume a larger role in the social research of the next decade: namely, making social relationships and social structures the units of statistical analysis.*

It is impossible to argue that this research at Columbia was independent of earlier work. First of all, Lazarsfeld had worked with Moreno and Jennings to develop a structural model of interpersonal choice (Moreno and Jennings, 1938). And Merton had been a graduate student at Harvard when the structural perspective was dominant there. Lazarsfeld (1975) described Merton's commitment to structural thought in these words, "Coming to the Bureau, he was asked to work on studies that certainly portrayed people as part of a social network and im-

---

[34]This work led to the concept of "Blau space" that is now standard in social network research (McPherson and Ranger-Moore, 1991).

[35]James Coleman, for example, taught Ronald Burt and Scott Feld. Peter Blau taught Danching Ruan and Terry C. Blum. And Charles Kadushin taught Gwen Moore and Richard Alba. All of these students became prominent contributors to social network analysis.

bedded in a historical context; but this was, so to say, taken for granted."

Thus, it is clear, then, that both Lazarsfeld and Merton had been exposed to structural thinking before they arrived at Columbia. But they were not the only ones; Duncan Luce was at Columbia in 1951 and Arnold Simmel moved from MIT to Columbia as a graduate student in 1952.[36] Both Luce and Simmel had been involved in the original Bavelas experiments at MIT.

My conclusion, then, is that although the Columbia effort was guided by the earlier work, it made important new contributions and added a great deal to the earlier approaches. The research at Columbia documented the importance of the structural approach by producing a whole series of new substantive findings. Columbia, moreover, was the first strictly sociological effort. It provided the model for a great many later developments in that field.

6.4 Iowa State University/Michigan State University in the mid 1950s

Some years after the unofficial demise of sociometry, there were a few younger scholars who rediscovered it. One of these was Everett M. Rogers. In the mid 1950s Rogers was a graduate student in rural sociology at Iowa State University where he received bachelors, masters and PhD degrees. For his dissertation, Rogers used some sociometric procedures in the study of the diffusion of innovations.

Rogers, shown in Figure 6.4, was born in the town of Carroll in western Iowa. In 1955, while working on his dissertation, he discovered the writings of Jacob Moreno. His data were produced by interviews with 155 Iowa farmers; he recorded information on the spread of several agricultural innovations. Rogers was looking for a way to uncover patterning in their spread. Faced with that problem, he concluded that Moreno's sociometric approach might be helpful. As he described it:

> *So I plotted the network links on a huge piece of paper*
> *(a map of the community), about 3 feet square. There*

---

[36]Luce and Coleman, moreover, shared an office during Luce's short tenure at Columbia.

was spatial clustering, but the sociogram was so busy, that little other pattern emerged. I spent the entire summer working with these data, and eventually tried using chemical colored balls and sticks to show the degree of opinion leadership of certain farmers, with the height and size of the ball indicating the number of sociometric nominations. Many people came to see my sociogram, but eventually I destroyed it, frustrated that I could not better understand the nature of the network. I did not think of using indices of density, etc. And computer programs were not yet available. I could not find any faculty member to help me with the problem, but I remember talking to several about it, and showing them my data.[37]

Rogers, then, discovered sociometry long after the general interest in it had waned. But, because he was unaware of some of the computational developments introduced by Katz and others, his first attempt was limited to the use of Moreno's graphical procedures. And it turned out that those graphical procedures did not provide the sort of analytic power that he was seeking.

But, because of his interest in diffusion, Rogers continued to think in structural terms. He worked with the idea of stages in the diffusion process and partitioned adopters in terms of when they embraced an innovation. He was later influenced by Lazarsfeld and his colleagues at Columbia, and began to produce sophisticated structural interpretations of his data on Iowa farmers. In a paper with Beal (Rogers and Beal, 1958) Rogers wrote:

An appropriate modification of Lazarsfeld's model (which he developed on the basis of his study of voting behavior) would be: technological farming ideas often flow from the impersonal sources to the innovators and early adopters and from them to the late majority and laggards.

After a few years teaching rural sociology at Ohio State University, Rogers went to work at Michigan State, this time in

---

[37]Personal communication.

Figure 6.4. Everett M. Rogers

the Department of Communication Science. He continued to work from a structural perspective and he turned out an impressive collection of students, many of whom have become important figures in social network analysis. Included among these are George Barnett, James Danowski, Richard Farace, Peter Monge, Nan Lin, and William Richards. These are all prominent contributors to social network research. Richards is currently the president of the International Network for Social Network Analysis.

Following his stint at Michigan State, Rogers moved to Stanford University where he worked with his student D. Lawrence Kincaid on a major network study in rural Korea (Rogers and Kincaid, 1981). And he continued his role as an educator by training Kincaid and another major contributor to network analysis, Ronald Rice. Thus, Rogers was, and continues to be, a major contributor to the field.

6.5 Manchester University/London School of Economics in the mid 1950s

In the 1920s and 30s British social anthropology had been dominated by two major figures, Bronislaw Malinowski and Alfred Reginald Radcliffe-Brown. Malinowski did display some interest in structural phenomena in his study of gift exchange in the Trobriand Islands (Malinowski, 1922). But it was Radcliffe-Brown—or R-B as he became known—who had a major impact on the development of a structural perspective. He is shown in Figure 6.5.

Radcliffe-Brown was born in Birmingham, England, in 1881. His father died when he was five, and his mother was left destitute. Alfred Brown (his name until he changed

Figure 6.5. Alfred Reginald Radcliffe-Brown

it at age forty-five) attended the Royal Commercial Travelers School in Middlesex until 1896 when he became a Foundation Scholar at King Edward's School. With financial support from his elder brother, he attended Trinity College, Cambridge. His performance was considered brilliant and he was awarded a college prize. From 1906 to 1908 he conducted fieldwork in the Andaman Islands. In 1909–1910 academic year he lectured at the London School of Economics. And in 1910 he returned to the field, this time in Australia.

In 1920 Radcliffe-Brown was awarded the newly created Chair of Social Anthropology at the University of Cape Town. From there he moved to the Anthropology Chair at Sydney.[38] And in 1930 he moved again—this time to the University of Chicago. He remained at Chicago until 1937 and overlapped with Warner, Davis, Whyte and Drake, who had all been involved in the earlier Harvard effort. At that point, he departed to become the first Chair in Social Anthropology at Oxford.

---

[38]One consequence of the move to Sydney was R-B's recruitment of W. Lloyd Warner, described in Chapter 3 above. In addition, at Sydney, Gregory Bateson worked under R-B's direction. Bateson went on to embrace a network perspective applied, for the most part, to cognitive structures (Bateson, 2002).

R-B was an admirer of Durkheim. He built from Durkheim's structural perspective and extended those ideas. In R-B's obituary, Firth (1956) commented on R-B's work in that area:

> As time went on, he developed the concept of social structure as a central theme in his analysis, and though he did not explore the concept itself systematically, he applied it with increasing success to the explanation of social phenomena. This success remains outstanding in the field of kinship, where the bulk of his contributions must remain as a part of the enduring fabric of anthropological studies.

As an eloquent spokesman for the structural perspective, Radcliffe-Brown had few peers. In the spring of 1937, the Dean of the Division of Social Sciences at Chicago organized a faculty seminar. One of the early speakers was Hutchins' neo-Thomist associate, Mortimer J. Adler. Adler presented the argument that psychology was the only possible social science. R-B asked for the opportunity to present a rebuttal. His request was granted and he presented his own lecture series published twenty years later, after his death, as *A Natural Science of Society* (Radcliffe-Brown, 1957).

In those lectures, R-B set out the foundations for the development of a natural science of society. Social relations were central in his thinking. He (1957, p.43) said, for example, "The relations *between* individuals in a social system are *social* relations." He (p. 44) generalized that idea and talked of social relations linking individual bees and ants into social structures. And he (p. 49) indicated that human society could be understood only, "by an investigation of human beings *arranged in a certain order*." It is evident, then, that R-B saw the full generality of the structural perspective.

Radcliffe-Brown went on to argue that in order to build a science based on the relations between people, we would need certain tools. As he (1957, p. 69) put it,

> A natural science is possible, first, wherever measurement can be applied to phenomena, and second, wherever relational analysis is possible, i.e., systems are

identifiable and characterizable. Relational analysis, even if not metrical, may be mathematical, in the sense that it will apply non-quantitative, relational mathematics. The kind of mathematics which will be required ultimately for a full development of the science of society will not be metrical, but will be that hitherto comparatively neglected branch of mathematics, the calculus of relations, which, I think, is on the whole more fundamental than quantitative mathematics.

In this statement Radcliffe-Brown anticipated exactly the developments that took place almost forty years later in the emerging field of social network analysis (Freeman, 1984a). His statement is an explicit description of the kinds of models that have been introduced to aid in the development of the field.[39]

For most of his career, R-B drifted from University to University, spreading the word about structural analysis. In their Foreword to R-B's book (1952), Evans-Pritchard and Eggan described his teaching, "He has taught social anthropology at Cambridge, London, Birmingham, Pretoria, Johannesburg, Cape Town, Sydney, Yenching, Oxford, Sao Paulo, Alexandria and Grahamstown, and in each of these places he is remembered with affection and respect."[40] Since he was always on the move, R-B never remained in any place long enough to produce students. He did work with Raymond Firth in Sydney and with Meyer Fortes at Oxford. It is evident that Firth and Fortes, along with the Indian sociologist, M. N. Srinivas, and the British social anthropologists, Edward E. Evans-Pritchard and Max Gluckman, considered themselves to be disciples of Radcliffe-Brown. All of them, particularly Evans-Pritchard (1940) and Gluckman, reflected R-B's structural approach in their own research.

Gluckman, then, owed his structuralist viewpoint to his exposure to Radcliffe-Brown (Cocks, 2001). Gluckman was originally South African, born in the Transvaal. He was a Rhodes

---

[39] These lectures were not widely available until their publication in 1957 after R-B's death. But R-B made similar pleas for structural thought in his presidential address to the Royal Anthropological Institute (Radcliffe-Brown, 1940) and in the introduction to his book on African kinship (Radcliffe-Brown and Forde, 1950).

[40] It is an interesting footnote that, although R-B taught at the University of Chicago with Eggan, Chicago is not among the institutions listed by Evans-Pritchard and Eggan.

Scholar at Oxford where he received his DPhil in 1936. He lectured at Oxford in the 40s, and in 1949 he was the founding Chair in the Department of Social Anthropology and Sociology at the University of Manchester. Gluckman is pictured in Figure 6.6.

In a personal communication, John Barnes described the Manchester Department:

*Figure 6.6. Max Gluckman, on the left,
with John Barnes*

*The Manchester department headed by Max Gluck-
man was indeed a very lively place in the early 1950s.
At a time when most British universities were short
of cash, Gluckman discovered a fund set up by Lord
Simon (a Manchester tycoon/philanthropist) for the
benefit of the social sciences of which even the other
social science departments in the Manchester social
science faculty seemed unaware. Gluckman was thus*

> *able to invite a lot of visitors, some just to give semi-*
> *nar papers, others for longer periods....George*
> *Homans gave a course of lectures which we all*
> *attended.*

The visitors at Manchester at that time included not only Homans, but a number of other structuralists and a few sociologists of other stripes. The structuralists included John Barnes, J. Clyde Mitchell, Elizabeth Bott and Sigfried Nadel. Barnes, Bott and Nadel were all working at the London School of Economics with which Manchester maintained a close relationship. The others included Edward Shils, Talcott Parsons and M. N. Srinivas.

Gluckman himself ran a regular seminar that was centered on structural issues (Mitchell, 1969, p. vi; Bott, 1971, p. 316). And at least partially as a result of Gluckman's influence, the works of this collection of British social anthropologists all displayed a structural perspective (Barnes, 1954; Bott, 1957; Gluckman, 1955; Mitchell, 1969; Nadel, 1957). Mitchell (along with his students) and Barnes both collected systematic structural data. Mitchell and Nadel both employed graphic images. And Nadel developed a primitive sort of algebraic system to model interpersonal role connections. Certainly, then, the Manchester/LSE group met all the conditions required to define their work as network analytic. They studied a wide range of structural phenomena, ranging from Bott's focus on social support and social control to Barnes' concern with friendship and kinship. And the fact that they all used the term "network" to refer to all of these kinds of linkages is evidence that they perceived the generality of their approach. Thus, these British social anthropologists must be counted among the contributors to the general social network paradigm. Their influence on subsequent work in the field was huge.

6.6 Massachusetts Institute of Technology in the late 1950s

In the late 1950s MIT experienced a rebirth as a place for network thinking and research—this time centered in the political science department. Although Bavelas and all of his students had left MIT by then, a new concern for social structural phenomena had developed among the political science faculty. The leaders of this new effort were Karl Wolfgang Deutsch and Ithiel de Sola Pool.

Karl Deutsch, shown in Figure 6.7, was born in Prague in 1912. He received his degree from the Deutsche Universitaet in

Prague in 1934. Then he went to law school at Charles University in Prague and received his law degree in 1938. A year later, Deutsch was awarded a fellowship to study at Harvard and came to the U.S. just ahead of the Nazi occupation. He was awarded his PhD in political science at Harvard in 1951.

Deutsch taught at MIT from 1945 to 1956. By all accounts, he was a remarkable teacher. According to one of his students in a graduate seminar on nationalism:[41]

Figure 6.7. Karl Deutsch

One day, as Karl spoke animatedly, Ruth (his wife) appeared at the door about five minutes after the 4 P.M. scheduled class adjournment. Karl saw her but kept talking. A few minutes later, Ruth took a couple of steps into the classroom. Karl kept talking, only faster. A few minutes later, Ruth walked up to the podium. Karl kept talking as fast as he could (which was very fast). Finally Ruth fumed to us, apologized for breaking up the class a half-hour past adjournment time, took Karl by the hand, pulled him out of the classroom, while explaining that they had to rush to meet their accountant to file their income tax. It was April 15.

---

[41]Reported in a memorial minute adopted by The Faculty of Arts and Sciences, Harvard University Samuel Beer, Stanley H. Hoffmann, Samuel P. Huntington, Robert O. Keohane, Sidney Verba, Jorge I. Dominguez, chairman.
(http://www.harvardsquarelibrary.org/unitarians/deutsch.html)

Deutsch was already thinking in structural terms in the 1940s. Harrison White reports that when he was a graduate student in physics at MIT in 1946 and 1947, he took an elective course with Deutsch. In that course he was introduced to a structural perspective in the study of social communication. By the mid 1950s Deutsch (1953) was using that structural perspective in the study of nationalism and information flow.

Deutsch's colleague Ithiel de Sola Pool was also interested in structural phenomena. Pool, shown in Figure 6.8, was born in New York City in 1917. His father, who had earned a PhD at Heidleberg University, came to New York from England. His mother was born in Palestine and was educated at Hunter College and the Sorbonne. Pool's father was a Rabbi and the leader of the New York Sephardic congregation.

Pool attended private school in New York and then went on to the University of Chicago, where he became the leader of the local Trotskyite party. His field was political science and he completed his PhD in 1952. A year later he began a career at MIT that continued until his death in 1984.

Pool's interest at MIT was in the patterns of acquaintance-ship and influence linking individuals. Pool wanted to build a formal model of those patterns, so he asked Deutsch about the possibility of locating a mathematician to help develop the appropriate mathematics. Deutsch had recently met a young mathematician, Manfred Kochen, who was working as a postdoc at Harvard. Deutsch introduced Kochen to Pool; they hit it off and began a long-term collaborative research effort.

Fred Kochen (as he called himself) was born in Vienna in 1928. His family barely managed to escape the

Figure 6.8. Ithiel de Sola Pool

Nazis by moving to New York. Fred attended the Brooklyn Technical High School and then attended MIT, where he received his bachelor's degree in physics in 1950. He went on to Columbia, where he completed his PhD in mathematics in 1955 and then moved to Harvard.

Kochen left Harvard in 1956 and took a job at the nearby IBM Thomas J. Watson Research Institute in Yorktown Heights, New York. So Pool and Kochen were able to continue their collaboration. In about 1958 they completed a manuscript on social contacts and social influence that they viewed as an early draft of a future book. They made a number of copies and circulated it to others whom they thought might be interested. It turned out to be a major contribution and was cited again and again both before and after it was published twenty years later (Pool and Kochen, 1978).

Even though it was unpublished, the Pool/Kochen paper introduced a good many students to the notion of the "small world."[42] In particular, it guided the work of Michael Gurevich's (1961) PhD thesis and Howard Rosenthal's (1960), B.S. thesis. Both were written under Pool's direction at MIT. In addition, Stanley Milgram (1967; Travers and Milgram, 1969), who was a graduate student at Harvard at the time, also drew on the Pool and Kochen paper in designing his dissertation on the small world phenomenon.

All three, Deutsch, Pool and Kochen, continued their structural work. According to his Harvard colleagues,[43] Deutsch described one of his later books (1963) as involving "the comparative study of many systems of communication and control, ranging from electronic computers to biological and nervous systems, and to human organizations and societies." Clearly, this statement displays a structural perspective.

Pool maintained his interest in communication. He went on to examine the structural properties and implications of the telephone (1977) and the internet (1983) for interpersonal communication. And, although he moved to Michigan in 1965, ac-

---

[42]Braun (2004) argues that the small world idea was introduced by a Hungarian novelist, Frigyes Karnithy, in 1929 in a short story called "Chains."

[43]Reported in the Harvard memorial minute cited above.

cording to Merrill Flood (cited in Garfield, 1989), "Fred (Kochen) partnered with Anatol Rapoport and Karl Deutsch and me," and worked primarily on information systems, but (perhaps through the influence of Rapoport and Deutsch) he retained his interest in social networks. As Flood put it, in the late 1980s Kochen was still concerned with "the evolution of social organs with mind-like properties, such as scientific communities (Kochen, 1986). All in all, it seems to me that this second MIT effort, focused on political issues, was yet another statement of the general social network perspective. Still, although it had some influence in political science and social psychology, it was not picked up by other social scientists.

6.7 Syracuse University in the late 1950s

In the late 1950s Morris H. Sunshine and I (who had been graduate students together at Northwestern) were both teaching at Syracuse University. Largely through the efforts of one of our colleagues, Warner Bloomberg, Jr., we obtained a multi-year Ford Foundation grant to study community decision-making in Syracuse.

I was born in Chicago in 1927. I grew up on the south side near the University of Chicago where my family had close ties. My father's lifelong best friend was Ralph Linton, for whom I was named. During my youth, Ralph was teaching at the University of Wisconsin and spent many of his weekends at our house. He was in touch with his colleagues at Chicago and through his visits we met most of the anthropologists there.

In addition, my mother, who was a Chicago alumna, was taking graduate work in political science at Chicago when I was a child. I recall, for example, being forced to sit through a seminar taught by the not-yet-Senator Paul Douglas when I was about seven years old. The seminar was undoubtedly excellent, but I don't seem to have retained much of its content.

I was exposed early in my life to a variety of structural influences. First, my father was a genealogist and constantly reminded me of the importance of familial relations. When I was sixteen I began college at Chicago. Then I served two years in the Navy, and after World War II, I switched to Roosevelt College in downtown Chicago. I chose Roosevelt mostly because St. Clair Drake (whom my family knew from his graduate student days at Chicago) was teaching there. Drake was my undergraduate mentor. He is pictured in Figure 4.6.

After all my years in academe, I still remember Drake as the best lecturer I ever heard. He would begin a fifty-minute lecture at, say, 9 A.M. The subject might be something like the difference between Malinowski's and Radcliffe-Brown's conceptions of function (both of which Drake systematically contrasted with the algebraic definition of function). There would be perhaps thirty-five students present at the beginning. At the end of the fifty minutes, Drake would typically be so wound up that he would not hear the class bell; he would lecture right on through it. One or two students might leave for other classes, but the rest of us would remain, spellbound. The lecture would continue right through the 10:50 bell, but at that point another lecturer and a new bunch of students would demand the classroom. So we would get up and work our way out into the hall, following Drake. His lecture never missed a beat. Most of the class would follow him very slowly down the hall, up three flights of stairs, and as far as his office door. We would stand there in the hall for maybe another hour; no one was willing to miss any part of Drake's extended lecture. It is no surprise to me that Ewart Thomas characterized him as the "preacher man" in his eulogy (Baber, 1999).

Drake had been an undergraduate student of Allison Davis. So he was hired to work on the Davis, Gardner and Gardner (1940) *Deep South* research. I learned about that project from him when I was his undergraduate student in the late 40s.

In 1952, while I was an MA student at the University of Hawaii, the geographer Forrest (Woody) Pitts was a junior faculty member and my neighbor in faculty-student housing. He introduced me to Hägerstrand's simulation studies of diffusion. At the same time, one of the young sociologists at Hawaii, Harry Ball, called my attention to the theoretical and experimental work done by Bavelas and Leavitt at MIT. These were all structural studies, though I was unable to see their similarity at the time.

In addition, Elizabeth Bott and I were close friends in the late 1940s, when she was an MA student at Chicago and I was still an undergraduate. She moved to England to complete her degree at the London School of Economics, but she and I arranged to meet at the 1956 sociology meetings in Detroit. So I learned about her study of families and social networks before the publication of her book (1957). And finally, in 1961, I read Rapoport's (1961) paper on random and biased nets. I was so impressed with his approach that I leaned on my graduate student, Fararo, to use Rapoport's model in his dissertation research (1963).

Morry Sunshine arrived at Northwestern one year after I did. Sunshine had grown up in Buffalo, New York. He attended the University of Missouri, where he studied history. As a graduate student he had switched to sociology and worked with Harry Ball, who had left Hawaii and was teaching at Missouri. Ball had decided that Sunshine would get better training at Northwestern University and persuaded him to transfer.

Sunshine and I both completed our PhDs at Northwestern. While he was there, Sunshine read some work by Moreno on sociometry, work by Robert Freed Bales on interaction process analysis and some of the social psychology coming out of the Michigan group. But like me, he failed at that time to make the connection among these several projects.

We were fortunate enough to be able to recruit a number of outstanding graduate students, including Thomas Fararo and Sue Freeman. And in 1968, working with Bloomberg and a political scientist, Stephen Koff, Sunshine and I designed a new approach to the study of community decision-making (Freeman, Bloomberg, Koff, Sunshine and Fararo, 1960; Freeman, Fararo, Bloomberg and Sunshine, 1962, 1963; Freeman, 1968).

Our perspective in that study was structural. We collected two-mode data on community decisions and decision-makers. Then we used principal components analysis to uncover the patterns of who participated with whom to solve community issues and which issues were linked in terms of attracting the same sets of participants.

It wasn't until the early 1960s—specifically when I read Rapoport's (1961) paper—that I was struck with what, for me, was a kind of epiphany. I suddenly saw that the works listed above—that by Davis, Gardner and Gardner, by Hägerstrand, by Bavelas and Leavitt, by Bott, and by Rapoport, and our own decision-making research—shared a common perspective; they all were structural. All were concerned with examining the patterning of links among social actors.

Fararo and Sunshine went on to use this same structural approach to examine social linkages among high school students (1964). And both Fararo (*circa* 1964) and I separately set out to specify the common mathematical properties of all of these seemingly different studies. Fararo circulated but never published his paper. Mine was presented several times and eventually published, but not until twenty-five years later (Freeman, 1989).

Here again, then, we have a collection of people who saw the generality of the social network approach. We designed a structural study of community decision-making. At the time we knew that it was a departure from the standard, individual-centered approach. But at the time we did not see its connection with other structural studies. It was not until our research was completed and Rapoport and Horvath published their article that we saw our work as reflecting a general structural perspective. So we did pioneer in applying the network perspective to research on community decision-making, and we were probably among the first sociologists to "discover" the work of the mathematical biologists at Chicago.[44]

The work reviewed in this chapter displayed all four of the elements that define contemporary social network analysis. This research all embodied rich structural intuitions. It all drew on data on social relations. It all produced images in the form of graphs and directed graphs. And it all developed either mathematical or computational models or both.

---

[44]Although Lazarsfeld was obviously aware of Rapoport; he invited him to be a fellow at the Center for Advanced Study in the Behavioral Sciences at Stanford the first year of its existence. Lazarsfeld, it should be remembered, was, himself, a mathematician as well as a sociologist.

Chapter 7

Social Network Analysis During the Dark Ages III: the 1960s

By the end of the 1950s enough structural research had been published so that any new network studies simply had to be derivative. Nevertheless, several research groups emerged in the 1960s that succeeded in broadening the perspective and introducing it to new audiences. Four such research groups will be reviewed in this chapter.

7.1 The Sorbonne in the early 1960s

In the late 1950s, a psychologist, Claude Flament, was working at the Laboratory of Experimental Psychology at the Sorbonne in Paris. He had been trained both in experimental psychology, by Paul Fraisse, and in mathematics, by Marc Barbut, Jean Marie Faverge and George Th. Guilbaut. At that time, he had read articles by Bavelas (1950) and Leavitt (1951) and had been inspired by them to conduct a series of experiments on group structure (Flament, 1956, 1958a, 1958b, 1961). He had also read Cartwright and Harary's (1956) paper on balance, and had found the little book on graph theory by Harary and Norman (1953). That inspired him to dig up the major work on graphs and hypergraphs by the French mathematician Claude Berge (1958). Flament followed up by contacting Berge and working with him in order to learn even more. So by the early 1960s he had become a master of graph theory.

In 1961, Flament was invited to participate in a summer program in Mathematics and the Social Sciences organized by Paul Lazarsfeld. At that time, James S. Coleman was editing a series of books on Mathematical Analysis of Social Behavior published by Prentice Hall. Coleman asked Flament to do a book for the series, and in 1963, Flament's book, *Applications of Graph Theory to Group Structure*, was published.

That book presented an integrated approach to both communication research and structural balance and presented applications on communication in work groups, on political blocs and on kinship structures. The book drew on structural data, and it included graphic images a well as both graph theoretic and algebraic models of structural phenomena. It was the complete package and leaves no doubt that Flament saw the whole social network picture. He drew on the work of other network analysts, but he produced what was perhaps the earliest general synthesis showing explicitly that a wide range of problems could all be understood as special cases of a general structural model. Today, Flament's work is widely recognized as foundational in the field.

7.2 University of Michigan in the mid 1960s

Edward O. Laumann, shown in Figure 7.1, received his PhD in sociology from Harvard in 1964. Azarian (2003) lists him as Harrison White's first Harvard PhD, and the implication is that Laumann's interest in social networks stemmed from that association. But although it is true that White did serve on Laumann's committee, he was a last-minute addition. Laumann's interest in networks arose from another source.

Laumann's regular long-term committee members were Talcott Parsons and George Homans. Parsons and Homans had both been students at Harvard during the period when Warner's structural perspective had dominated. And Homans, particularly, had embraced that perspective. So as a graduate student at Harvard, Laumann learned about Warner's earlier work on stratification. And like Arensberg and Chapple before him, Laumann set out to adopt the Warner approach and to make it more systematic. His aim was to "devise a more rigorous empirical test of the differentiation of social classes as interacting social circles or groups."[45]

Laumann went on to produce social network research focused on stratification (Laumann 1973; Laumann and Guttman, 1966; Laumann and Pappi, 1973, 1976), politics (Laumann and Knoke, 1987), and most recently on sexual behavior (Laumann, Gagnon, Michael and Michaels, 1994). At the same time, he played a major role in training students

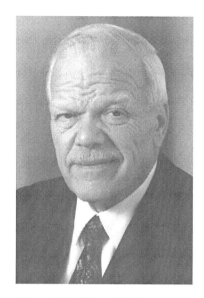

Figure 7.1. Edward O. Laumann

both at Michigan and later at the University of Chicago. A number of his former students have themselves become leaders in social network research. Among them are Stephen Berkowitz, Ronald Burt, Joseph Galaskiewicz, Alden Klovdahl, David Knoke, Peter Marsden, Martina Morris, David Prensky and Philip Schumm.

7.3 University of Chicago in the late 1960s

In the 1960s both Peter Blau and James A. Davis were teaching in the Sociology Department at the University of Chicago. Blau was born in Vienna in 1918. He had received his PhD from the Columbia Sociology Department. According to Blau, Georg Simmel, Talcott Parsons, Robert Merton and Paul Lazarsfeld had all drilled into him the importance of thinking structurally. Heeding their advice, he had already begun his life-long commitment to developing a structural approach in sociology (Blau and Duncan, 1967; Blau and Schoenherr, 1971).

---

[45]Personal communication.

Davis received his PhD from Harvard and went to work at Chicago in 1957. So although Davis was too late for the structural thrust at Harvard, students that he and Blau shared succeeded in passing Blau's structural focus on to him. In addition, he was influenced in this direction by his association with Harrison White, who was his colleague at Chicago from 1959 until 1963.

By the late 1960s Davis was interested in Heider's (1946) ideas about balance. He was particularly taken with Cartwright and Harary's (1956) graph theoretic treatment of those ideas. So he found Ore's (1963) book and learned some graph theory. The result was an important paper (Davis, 1967) that generalized the idea of balance from a cognitive to a social structural context. At the same time, Davis worked with his graduate student Sam Leinhardt (Davis and Leinhardt, 1971), and began developing a series of formal models dealing with transitivity in social relations (Davis, 1970).

Clearly, this work reflects an awareness of the generality of the social network paradigm. It is clear that both Blau and Davis were influenced by others, particularly by the Michigan and the Columbia groups. But each of these Chicago sociologists made important contributions. And both had long-range impact on the development of social network analysis.

7.4 The University of Amsterdam in the late 1960s

Robert Mokken was a principal figure in a development that took place at the University of Amsterdam in the late 1960s. Mokken had been trained in mathematical statistics. He had been working on problems of mass communication and had read structural studies by Katz and Lazarsfeld (1955), Everett Rogers (1962) and Harary, Norman and Cartwright (1965).

Mokken was teaching at the University of Amsterdam and working in the University's Mathematics Center. At the Center, he developed a collaboration with a computer programmer, Jac Anthonisse, who specialized in graph theory and operations research. And at the same time, he began working with a graduate student, Frans Stokman.

In 1968, when Mokken moved into the Faculty of Political Science, these three started a study of interlocking directorates in the Netherlands that ended up creating a major stir in the Dutch national press (Helmers, Mokken, Plijter, Stokman and Anthonisse, 1975). Stokman described what happened:

> *A leftist Catholic magazine "De Nieuwe Linie" published the results of our study in its issues of December 23 and 30, 1971 under the heading: "The Banks have the Power in The Netherlands, not Parliament". An incredible amount of publicity came over us with a broad coverage by newspapers, radio and TV. However, completely opposed to our intention and our main message, the journalists emphasized the new list of names of persons…A TV spot of the Pacifist Socialist Party showed each of the names in succession. While the one name was coming up from the left and the other name shifted away to the right, a phone bell jingled. We were invited for interviews, sometimes with "network persons" themselves, among whom [was] the President of the ABN-AMRO Bank, the person with the highest rush.[46] Several groups demanded a nation wide discussion. This resulted in a conference on January 19th, 1972 in the meeting room of the Second Chamber of Parliament. Four groups were invited: captains of industry and the financial sector, the trade unions, politicians, and social scientists.*

Thus a major network analytic study had an important impact on Dutch politics.

A second line of research started at the same time was focused on group formation in the United Nations and led to Stokman's dissertation (1977). Stokman and Anthonisse, moreover, developed a set of computer programs designed to facilitate the use of graph theory in the analyses of structural data. All of this work embodied structural intuitions. All of it generated relation-based data, produced graphic images and generated graph theoretic models.

---

[46]The concept of "rush" in Stokman's description of the political consequences of their research was developed by Anthonisse (1971) as a general algorithm for betweenness-based centrality.

It is clear, then, that this Dutch group saw the generality of their structural approach. They defined a general graph theoretic model that specified each research application simply as a special case of their general model. The impact of this work was apparent in northern Europe almost immediately and was later recognized throughout the world.

7.5 The Dark Ages: Retrospect and Prospect

Neither the Harvard group nor the Moreno group working in the 1920s and 30s had succeeded in spreading a generalized social network perspective to the wider social science community. Yet from the 1940s through the 1960s, other investigators—sometimes more or less independently—came up with a structural perspective and conducted research that embodied the network approach. In the last three chapters I have reviewed fourteen settings in which such work was done. The obvious question, then, is why none of these other efforts succeeded in spreading the word about network research to a broad enough audience to provide a generalized paradigm for social network analysis.

The efforts of the social psychologists led by Lewin certainly had a major impact, but it was apparently limited to the field of social psychology. It is true that the Bavelas experiment did generate immediate cross-disciplinary interest. But its impact dwindled when subsequent investigators lost sight of the generality of the earlier work at MIT. The formal models published by Cartwright and Harary and the theories and data sets produced by Festinger and Newcomb and their students certainly attracted the attention of other social psychologists, but they were not recognized by many people working in other social science fields.

The Michigan State group, led by Loomis, collected a great deal of important structural data in communities throughout the world. But basically, the Michigan State group simply refined and extended the sociometric approach. Therefore, I suspect that they were casualties of the general abandonment of sociometry.

The work of Lévi-Strauss and Weil inspired kinship analysts but failed to arouse the interest of others in the social science community. Rashevsky's group at Chicago was too mathematical to catch the imagination of most social scientists.[47] Hägerstrand also had a large impact, but seemingly only in the community of social geographers.

The Lazarsfeld-Merton group at Columbia produced a great deal of structural research. They began, I think, to lay the foundations for the development of a growing interest in the structural approach among sociologists. The Coleman, Katz and Menzel (1957) study of the diffusion of a medical innovation was particularly important in terms of its impact on sociologists generally.

Everett Rogers at Iowa State, and later at Michigan State, defined a structural approach to the study of diffusion and went on to play a major part in the creation a new social science specialty, communication science. For the most part, however, his influence was limited to students of communication. Similarly, the structural research centered at Manchester and the London School seems primarily to have influenced others in the field of anthropology.

The Deutsch-Poole group in political science at MIT contributed to the growing awareness of the importance of network thinking among political scientists. The Syracuse group was too peripheral to have had much impact but we may have increased the general level of awareness of structural thinking among those interested in community decision-making.[48]

Flament at the Sorbonne used his knowledge of graph theory to unify the early MIT and later Columbia research efforts. In addition, he showed the potential of structural modeling to the community of social psychologists working in Europe. Edward Laumann built on the early work at Harvard and along with Louis Guttman, extended that approach to the study of large communities. Blau brought the structuralism developed at Columbia to the University of Chicago. He influenced Davis, and

---

[47] In fact, the only sociologist I have found who published in the *Bulletin of Mathematical Biophysics* is Leo Goodman (1952). And Goodman is not a typical sociologist; he is a mathematical statistician.

[48] I recall receiving phone calls at that time from both Pete Rossi and Jim Coleman expressing interest in our approach.

their work added yet again to the general level of awareness of structural research, particularly among sociologists. And finally, the Amsterdam group had an important impact, especially in promoting structural thinking among sociologists in northern Europe.

The overall pattern, then, seems to be one in which each succeeding contribution introduced a new segment of the social science community to the structural perspective. But, at the end of the 1960s, no version of network analysis was yet universally recognized as providing a general paradigm for social research. By then, however, the broad community of people engaged in social research were ready to embrace a structural paradigm. It was in this setting that Harrison White and his students began their structural work. The next chapter will examine their contributions.

Chapter 8

The Renaissance at Harvard

Finally we return to Harvard, this time to the unique contributions of Harrison Colyer White and his students. White was born in Washington, D.C., in 1930 to an old Southern family. His father was a career navy physician, and White's youth was spent moving from navy base to navy base. As he described it (MacLean and Olds, 2001):

> *Although I am a Southerner, I don't sound like it, I went to first grade in Nashville, which was our home city, and I was back there a lot, as I had endless relatives and grandparents, but I always lived in port cities. New Orleans, Long Beach, San Francisco, Philadelphia, Norfolk, you name the navy bases and I was there. And so I went to—I think—seven or eight grammar schools and three high schools.*

White dates his structural interest from his mother's early emphasis on the importance of both status and kinship. As he put it (MacLean and Olds, 2001):

> *My mother was very oriented to her—both her—lines of descent, but also I had lots of aunts and uncles, and you keep track of all the cousins, and my middle name Colyer is my great uncle Arthur Colyer who was editor of the Nashville Banner. And then—from my mother's point of view it was important—my name*

> *"Harrison" was a family name. There were a couple*
> *of presidents up in our family tree...And so there was*
> *all this kind of mixture of kinship ties and relational*
> *things, but also a sensitivity to status and control and*
> *power and so on. So I think that's both what got me*
> *into sociology and what's shaped what I try to do in it.*

His mother made much of the fact that he was named "Harrison" for the two presidents, William Henry Harrison and Benjamin Harrison, who were both her kinsmen.

White entered Massachusetts Institute of Technology as a fifteen-year-old freshman. He studied mathematics and science (crystallography) and went on to complete his PhD in theoretical physics in 1955. As an undergraduate at MIT he learned the appropriate mathematical tools for structural analysis by taking courses in electrical engineering and operations research. As a graduate student, he took Karl Deutsch's course on nationalism and learned that the same structural perspective could be applied to social phenomena. So his PhD in physics provided him with sound mathematical skills and his exposure to Deutsch contributed to his developing interest in social structure.

White's first job was in the Operations Research Office at Johns Hopkins University. But after one year, his interest in social science led him to go to the Stanford Center for Advanced Study in Behavioral Sciences. There he met Harold Guetzkow, who was teaching at the Carnegie Institute of Technology. Through that contact, White met Guetzkow's Carnegie Tech colleague, the Nobel laureate in economics Herbert Simon. Guetzkow and Simon were apparently impressed with White because they invited him to join them at Carnegie Tech in Pittsburgh.

White taught at Carnegie Tech for two years, from 1957 until 1959. While he was there, he enrolled as a graduate student in sociology at Princeton. He chose Princeton because they had a residence requirement of only one year and he had already "had enough of graduate school." In any case, while he taught at Carnegie Tech, he also earned a second PhD in 1960 at Princeton. His dissertation in sociology was a social network study that involved the application of algebra in modeling organizational behavior.

In 1959 James S. Coleman left the Sociology Department at the University of Chicago to start a new department at Johns Hopkins University. Coleman had been teaching mathematics-oriented courses in sociology at Chicago, so the Chicago Chairman, Phillip Hauser, set out to find a replacement who was also skilled in mathematics. He found Harrison White, who at the time was almost finished with his PhD in sociology. With his mathematical training as a physicist, White was a natural candidate and he got the job.

As the department's new mathematical guru, White was assigned the job of teaching sociological statistics. He did, but when the course was over, one of the brighter students characterized it as "fascinating, in the sense of seeing a subject matter taught by its worst enemy."[49] What that student saw was that White did not think like the standard survey sociologist. Even at the beginning of his career White thought in structural terms.

White continued teaching at Chicago until 1963. During that time he extended the earlier work of Lévi-Strauss and Weil and developed an elegant structural model of kinship (1963). At the same time he began working with Morris Friedell to produce a model of vacancy chains that was designed to account for social mobility. This early work focused on careers in the Episcopal church.

In 1963 R. Freed Bales arranged for White to receive an offer from Harvard. White accepted and moved to Cambridge. There he continued to apply the structural perspective to a range of problems. His work on vacancy chains continued and resulted in a book (1970).

At Harvard, White taught a number of courses and seminars on subjects like stratification, mathematical models and complex organizations. But perhaps his greatest impact began in 1965 when he taught a low-level undergraduate course, "An Introduction to Social Relations, 10." Mullins and Mullins (1973, p. 255) described it:

---

[49]This response was reported to me in a personal communication from Joel Levine, who knew the student who is being quoted.

> *That course has to be one of the few introductory cours-*
> *es ever taught which, at completion, had almost as*
> *many graduate as undergraduate students attending*
> *lectures faithfully.*

At the same time, White produced a notable series of papers on blockmodeling with his students Scott A. Boorman,
Ronald L. Breiger and Gregory H. Heil (White, Boorman and
Breiger, 1976; Boorman and White, 1976; Heil and White, 1976).
His paper on structural equivalence with another graduate student, François Lorrain (Lorrain and White, 1971), has become a
cornerstone of the field (Michaelson, 1990). All of this work displays White's complete mastery of the application of formal tools
to the study of social networks. Azarian (2000) credits that mastery to White's training in physics:

> *At one level White's original training in, and contin-*
> *ued contact with, the world of physics finds a clear*
> *expression in his recurrent references to, and even*
> *borrowings from, physicists' models in studying so-*
> *cial structures and processes, indicating that it is the*
> *schooling in theoretical physics rather than in classi-*
> *cal sociology which, at least initially, provides the main*
> *frame of reference in his analysis of social phenomena.*
> *White's works, especially the early ones, are abundant*
> *in examples. One is to be found in a paper on model-*
> *ing stochastic processes from 1962 where he holds that*
> *"elementary events such as (individuals' arrival at*
> *and departure from spontaneously formed and un-*
> *structured casual groups as in cocktail parties) can*
> *most conveniently be thought of as inherently ran-*
> *dom events governed by laws analogous to those fol-*
> *lowed in radioactive decay processes." Or, in 1964 he*
> *writes: "(i)t should be possible eventually to find par-*
> *allels between kinship structures…and modem ac-*
> *counts of the atomic structure of magnetic crystals*
> *and of electronic switching circuitry."*

> *More, in an article from 1971 jointly written with*
> *Lorrain, White seeks to develop a more adequate ac-*

count of complex social structures and maintains that,
in pondering over "how to get at the interweaving of
pair relations into the complex tapestry of social struc-
ture and process, the theory of electric circuits comes
to mind as an analogue..."

Whether he drew on physics or not, there is absolutely no doubt that all of White's work has consistently embodied the complete social network paradigm. His work serves as a model for research in social network analysis. But, perhaps White's greatest contribution has been in his role as a teacher. He indoctrinated a whole generation of Harvard students with a structural perspective. At his festschrift in San Diego in 1997, Joel Levine, one of his earliest Harvard students, and Kathleen M. Carley, one of his latest, presented a joint paper titled "On with the Revolution." In it they constructed an image of what it was like to be a student at Harvard during the period when the network analytic renaissance was taking place:

Once upon a time when the world was young, in the
shrouded beginnings of history—circa 1960–1970—
structuralism or "network" research was a dubious
venture, something done primarily by young people,
done by risk takers at the fringe of the sociological es-
tablishment. And there was a sociological establish-
ment. Unlike today there was a high status self-assured
center of the profession, some kind of ill-defined "grand
theory" or "structural-functionalism." And there was
a quantitative fringe of the profession centered, pri-
marily, on survey research, also very self-assured.
Theoreticians had not succeeded in creating "theory"
as that word was recognized by natural sciences. But,
within their self-assured circle, they had solved that
problem by redefining the word: Instead of moving
their work toward theory they had moved the word
"theory" toward their work. In this jungle landscape
of grand theory versus positivism, structuralism was
an insignificant creature. Structuralists certainly saw
themselves as intellectuals, but didn't trust grand the-
ory. Structuralists had the formal mathematical skills

of the positivists, but saw the positivists as misguided "reductionists" analyzing individual behavior, separated it from the "structures" that shaped individual behavior into social behavior.

And then, somehow, something happened. Harrison assembled the most enjoyable, intellectually diverse, and most productive work groups I've ever seen. The work was abetted by the simultaneous birth of cheap computing, by late nights, and by the central figure, Harrison, and something happened. To understand what Harrison did as the central figure there is a good analogy in a famous observation of Thomas Jefferson's. Jefferson applauded the culture of the rural farmer as compared to the corruption of the urban dweller. But the reason for this, Jefferson argued, was that the farmer succeeded by beating nature whereas the city dweller succeeded by beating other men. In this group that Harrison attracted, we succeeded by beating nature. And something happened.

Actually lots of somethings happened. The one that is remembered is CONCOR. But there were lots of things, remembered now mainly by members of this group: Semi-group algebras, homomorphic reductions, image tables, dictionaries, the first letter / last letter law. A methodological problem for which there was no method, the need for a procedure that could "organize" the data from a group as large five, fifteen, or fifty people was solved. As a practical computation problem, the solution became routine. That certainly did not complete the revolution but after this work one of Kuhn's pigeonholes had at least one pigeon: A method to fit the unit of analysis and the attributes of the unit. What grew out of that group and out of the much larger group in the profession as a whole is more than CONCOR. Probably the real base of the disci-

> *pline that has grown in the following generation is the use of structural ideas to make sense out of field work and primary and secondary data analyses where the new ideas make sense.*

Clearly, Harvard was a pretty exciting place to be during that period. The setting was intellectually stimulating and the students were outstanding. Together they made Harvard the center of structural research.

Abbott (1994) described White's reputation "As a man who has started sociological revolutions, introduced new techniques, and trained one of the finest groups of students in the discipline." The last feature, training students, is perhaps White's greatest strength. A list of White's students is a virtual who's who in social network analysis. Almost all of his PhDs have published in the social network area. Although some have not continued as network analysts, a number of them remain at the forefront of the field. The active network analysts include Peter Bearman, Paul Bernard, Phillip Bonacich, Ronald L. Breiger, Kathleen M. Carley, Ivan Chase, Bonnie Erickson, Claude S. Fischer, Mark Granovetter, Joel Levine, Siegwart M. Lindenberg, Barry Wellman and Christopher Winship.

From the beginning, White saw the broad generality of the structural paradigm, and he managed to communicate both that insight and his own enthusiasm to a whole generation of outstanding students. Certainly the majority of the published work in the field has been produced by White and his former students. Once this generation started to produce, they published so much important theory and research focused on social networks that social scientists everywhere, regardless of their field, could no longer ignore the idea. By the end of the 1970s, then, social network analysis came to be universally recognized among social scientists.

But White and his students were not the only ones who could lay claim to the social network approach. As we saw in Chapters 3 through 7, a relatively large number of other investigators had already come up with essentially the same synthesis. In fact, a general social network perspective was employed in no less than seventeen centers by seventeen collections of scholars over the forty-year period from the late 1930s through the late 1970s.

Of course the developments at these several centers were not all independent of one another. Those that emerged later undoubtedly drew on the work of at least some of the earlier efforts. By the time that Davis and Blau worked at Chicago, Mokken at Amsterdam and White and his students at Harvard, it is clear that any contributions they made stood on the foundations already established by Moreno, Warner, Lewin, Lévi-Strauss and Weil, Rashevsky, Hägerstrand, Lazarsfeld and Merton, Radcliffe-Brown and Gluckman, Flament, Pool and Kochen, Freeman and Sunshine, Rogers, and Laumann. Nonetheless, each of the later efforts introduced some new aspect of social network analysis and cast some new light on the whole enterprise.

On the other hand, it is likely that some of the earlier efforts were somewhat independent. The individuals involved form a diverse collection with very different backgrounds. They represent five different nations (France, Great Britain, the Netherlands, Sweden and the United States) and seven different disciplines (anthropology, social psychology, geography, mathematical biology, sociology, political science and experimental psychology). The individuals involved—coming from different countries and representing different disciplines—could each lay at least partial claim to having developed their own social network paradigm. Those involved in any of the earlier efforts could argue their work was a precursor to the work at Harvard.

The literature on the sociology of science (Kuhn, 1962; McCann, 1978; Mullins and Mullins, 1973) suggests that the expected outcome of competition about who initiated what is usually rancor. The competing claimants would be expected to bicker and quibble, and engage in endless conflict. But, as we shall see in Chapter 9, this conflict did not occur. Instead, these several claimants came together and formed a single organized collectivity. In Chapter 9, I will try to sort out some of the forces that led to this organization.

Chapter 9

Getting Organized

Writing in the early 1970s, Mullins and Mullins (1973, p. 264) described social network analysis up to that point in time as "...random pieces sitting out in the desert (forest?) of sociological knowledge." This description is consistent with the argument I have been developing in the preceding four chapters. I have proposed that the years between 1940 and the late 1960s witnessed the emergence of a large number of potentially competing "schools" of social network analysis. If that argument is true, then the field should have been pretty well fragmented in the 1970s.

In an attempt to explore this issue, I canvassed the founders—the participants in the various syntheses listed in the earlier chapters. I was able to interview twenty-one of them about their own introductions to structural thinking. Each was asked two questions: "Were you influenced by any particular pieces of literature, teachers, colleagues, post docs, students?" and "What literature or what people?"

The results give strong support to the notion that the field was fragmented. Sixty-eight influentials were mentioned. Of those, forty-nine were mentioned only once. Of the thirteen who were mentioned more than once, ten were mentioned twice, and only three had three or more mentions. Moreno had six, Harary had four, and Bavelas had three. Thus, the overwhelming tendency of the early social network analysts was to generate unique idiosyncratic lists of others who they claimed had influenced their network thinking. There was no common agreement about intellectual antecedents.

But beyond the sheer numbers, the patterning of answers is revealing. The answers were analyzed using the Kamada-Kawai spring-embedder in the program, PAJEK.[50] That algorithm is a form of multidimensional scaling that locates points in such a way that connected points are close and unconnected points are far apart. The resulting image of influence is displayed in Figure 9.1. Individuals who were interviewed are shown in black. All others are grey.

The picture reveals a huge hole that separates the cluster on the right from the smaller one on the left. The two clusters are bridged by Karl Deutsch, a political scientist, and James S. Coleman, a sociologist. With the exception of one mathematician, Øystein Ore, everyone to the left of the gap is a sociologist. Those on the right are an eclectic hodgepodge made up of anthropologists, geographers, social psychologists, communication scientists, political scientists, historians and mathematicians, and only a small handful of sociologists.[51]

Although they are almost all sociologists, the individuals on the left are only loosely linked; they each tend to name different influentials. In contrast, although they represent several disciplines, those on the right are more closely linked; they show more agreement about patterns of influence. This structural form suggests that there was a major gap between most mainstream sociologists and the individuals from other fields. The sociologists, it seems, came from a different intellectual background and displayed less consensus about the origins of their ideas about social network analysis.

---

[50] PAJEK is a network analysis and display program written by Vladimir Batagelj and Andrej Mrvar. It is distributed free for noncommercial use at:

http://vlado.fmf.uni-lj.si/pub/networks/pajek/

[51] The sociologists on the right are George Lundberg, Robert F. Winch, Harry V. Ball, Morris H. Sunshine, Thomas J. Fararo, Sue C. Freeman and me. Winch and Ball were Sunshine's and my teachers, and Fararo and Sue Freeman were Sunshine's and my students. Both Sunshine and I have always considered ourselves to be a multidisciplinary scholars. Lundberg is the only sociologist in this list who was not nominated by Sunshine and me.

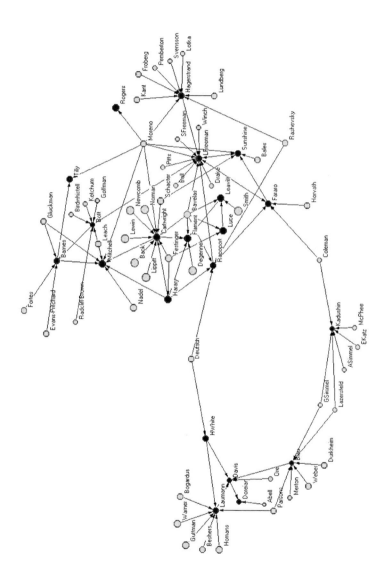

Fig. 9.1. Influences on some founders of social network analysis

Interestingly enough, this interpretation, based on retro-spective data collected in the late 1990s, is supported by evidence from an earlier study. In 1978, Sue Freeman and I were involved in a study of the impact of a computer network on the organization of social network research (Freeman and Freeman, 1980; Freeman, 1984b). Forty individuals, all of whom worked as social network analysts, were linked by computer. The system was call "Electronic Information Exchange System (EIES) and worked very much like today's internet.

Before they were linked by computer, we presented each participant with a network questionnaire. Each was given a list of participants, and each was asked to rate each of the others on the following scale:

4 - Close personal friend
3 - Friend
2 - Person I've met
1 - Person I've heard of, but not met
0 - Unknown name

Then, after eight months of internet connection, the same questionnaire was administered again. All in all, thirty-four individuals responded both times.

The two sets of data permitted the study of changes in interpersonal ties during the eight months of computer linkage. We stacked the two matrices—before and after—normalized to remove the effects of differences in row and column totals and entered the combined data into a standard singular-value decomposition program.[52] This analysis showed the changes in the social linkages between pairs of network analysts that occurred during the eight-month period.

The initial proximities are shown in Figure 9.2. The fact that the individuals are widely spread out suggests that the network community lacked a coherent structure in 1978. Individuals are grouped in a way that might indicate the presence of two loose clusters, but their boundaries are certainly not clear.

---

[52]Singular-value decomposition simply places actors with similar patterns of response in close proximity while those with dissimilar patterns are separated. The UCINET program was used.

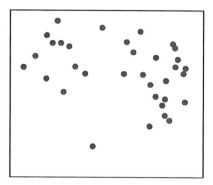

Figure 9.2. Social proximities at the start of the EIES research

The real message comes through when we examine the patterning of changes over the eight-month period. According to the direction of their movement, the points fall into four distinct categories. Some moved greater distances and some small-

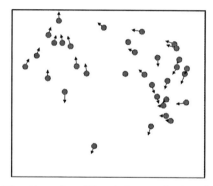

Figure 9.3. Direction of positional change during the EIES research

er distances, but their movements over the eight months fall into four distinct classes. The directions points moved are shown in Figure 9.3 and their final locations are shown in Figure 9.4.

Points in Figure 9.4 are marked according to the direction they moved. Those that moved up and to the left are white. Those that moved down and to the right are black. Those that dropped toward the lower left are marked with a cross. And the two points that did not move at all are grey.

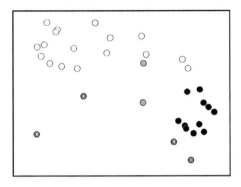

Figure 9.4. Final locations of individuals in the EIES research

It turns out that each of the markings identifies a relatively well-defined and fairly homogeneous collection of individuals. The pair shaded grey had done a great deal of early network research. Thus, they were already well known, but they did not participate in the experimental internet connection at all. Those marked with a cross were neophytes who did not participate and actually dropped out of network research during the eight-month period. White points represent individuals from several fields who at that time were using the computer hookup to get organized. They formed the core of a collaborative, interdisciplinary social-networks community. In contrast, the black points were sociologists who objected to forming a new specialty and who were anxious to define network research simply as a subarea in the discipline of sociology.

Like the earlier picture of retrospective influence, the picture of social cohesion in 1978 shows most of the sociologists as distinctly separate from the rest of the interdisciplinary, social-networks community. It is really remarkable that two totally different kinds of questions, put more than twenty years apart and analyzed by different procedures, could produce such similar results. The split between the sociologists and the others, it would seem, was so robust that it appears no matter how the data are collected and analyzed. And, like the image of influence, this picture of social proximity shows a fragmented collection of individuals.

Overall, then, given the several separate "schools" of network analysis and given the split shown above, it would be reasonable to expect that some kind of conflict might have emerged among the competing claimants to the network idea. Yet, although there were some minor skirmishes in the 1970s, no major conflicts have ever taken place. Instead, the representatives of each of these network "schools" have all joined together and organized themselves into a single coherent field. The present chapter will examine how this was done.

One reason for the lack of conflict was probably the result of the central place of mathematics in the development of the field (Wolfe, 1978; Freeman, 1984a; Hummon and Carley, 1993). Among the people who have done social network research, many actually earned formal degrees in mathematics. These include Vladamir Batagelj, Irénée Bienaymé, Michael Copobianco, Martin Everett, Ove Frank, Maureen T. Hallinan, Mark Handcock, Frank Harary, Paul Holland, Manfred Kochen, Michael Ikeda, Eugene Johnsen, Leo Katz, John Kemeny, Herbert Landahl, Hyman Landau, Paul Lazarsfeld, Duncan Luce, John Molluzzo, Juhani Nieminen, Robert Norman, Charles Proctor, Willard Quine, Anatol Rapoport, Karl Reitz, Gery Sabidussi, Alfonso Shimbel, Steve Seidman, Ray Solomonoff, J. Laurie Snell, Tom Snijders, David Strauss, Steven Strogatz, Gerald Thompson, Stanley Wasserman, Henry Watson and André Weil.

Others, like Peter Killworth, François Lorrain, Alexander Macfarlane, Mark Newman, Nicolas Rashevsky, Derek De Solla Price, Steve Strogatz, Duncan Watts and Harrison White, were all trained in mathematical physics. And still others, like Phipps Arabie, William Batchelder, Scott Boorman, John Boyd, Ron Breiger, Carter Butts, Jim Coleman, Pat Doreian, Tom Fararo, Anuska Ferligoj, Claude Flament, Louis Guttman, Martina Morris, Philippa Pattison, John Roberts, Andrew Seary, Herb Simon and Chris Winship are all social scientists but could easily pass as mathematicians. This means that, from the start, contributions to social network analysis were often couched in mathematical terms. The relative precision of these mathematical treatments gave social networks an advantage. Because of that precision, the network field did not generate the same kinds of quibbles and misunderstandings over terms and concepts that lead to conflict in fields that are wedded to a natural language (Freeman, 1960, 1984a).

Beyond this mathematical precision, the unification of the many separate strands of network analysis is the result of a great deal of integrative work by a number of individuals and institutions. There seem to have been eight ways in which various individuals and institutions acted as integrators: (1) Some moved from place to place and in so doing, bridged diverse collections of social network scholars. (2) Some produced computer programs that standardized the analysis of social network data. (3) Some organized conferences designed explicitly to bring previously separate groups together. (4) One created an organization designed explicitly to link social network researchers worldwide. (5) One started a journal aimed at centering the literature in the field. (6) One arranged to use an early kind of internet to connect people doing social network research. (7) Working together, some established a series of regular annual meetings. (8) And finally, UCI, the University of California at Irvine, played a special role in unifying the social network community. These will all be examined in the following sections.

9.1 Movement and Bridging

In the previous chapters I have described a good deal of bridging among early practitioners of social network analysis. In the first place, there was the famous (or infamous) series of face-to-face meetings between Kurt Lewin (along with an unnamed collection of his students) and Jacob Moreno in 1935. These meetings may have resulted in at least some modifications in Lewin's perspectives about research.

But most bridging occurred as a consequence of faculty and student migration. As people working on social networks moved from place to place among the several main network research centers discussed in Chapters 3 through 7, they built bridges between "schools" of network analysis. Movements linking the main research centers are shown in Figure 9.5. In the figure, asterisks—like the one following White's move from MIT to Chicago in 1959—represent indirect moves. They involve intermediate transfers to institutions other than the ones shown

When	Who	From	To
1934	Arensberg	Harvard	MIT
1935	Warner Gardner A. Davis Drake	Harvard	Chicago
1940	Whyte	Harvard	Chicago
1942	Deutsch	Harvard	MIT
1948	Festinger Cartwright Kelley Thibaut Schachter	MIT	Michigan
1950	Simmel	MIT	Harvard
1951	Back Luce Luce Simmel	MIT MIT Michigan Harvard	Columbia* Michigan Columbia MIT
1952	Simmel	MIT	Columbia
1953	Homans Pool	Harvard Chicago	Manchester MIT
1954	Deutsch Homans	MIT Manchester	Chicago* Harvard
1955	Rapoport	Chicago	Michigan
1956	Coleman	Columbia	Chicago
1959	White	MIT	Chicago*
1960	Deutsch	Chicago	MIT
1961	Deutsch	MIT	Harvard
1963	White	Chicago	Harvard
1964	Laumann	Harvard	Michigan

Figure 9.5. Migrations linking social network research centers

in the table. White, for example, actually left MIT for Johns Hopkins University in 1955. He spent the 1956–57 year at the Center for Advanced Study in the Behavioral Sciences at Stanford. Then he moved from Hopkins to the Carnegie Institute of Technology in 1957. He finally arrived at the University of Chicago in 1959.

The table shows that moves were frequent. They were particularly frequent between Harvard and both MIT and Chicago, and between MIT and Michigan. It is likely that movements of these kinds helped to integrate the several potentially competing "schools" of social network analysis.

In addition, a good many early structuralists spent time together at the Center for Advanced Study in the Behavioral Sciences at Stanford. Paul Lazarsfeld, who had been involved in both Moreno's sociometry and the social network research effort at Columbia, was a major figure in the creation of the Center (Luce, 1978, p. 268). When the Center started in 1955 then, four structuralists, Bavelas from MIT; Lazarsfeld from Columbia; Luce from MIT, but then working at Columbia; and Rapoport from the mathematical biology group at Chicago, were among its initial fellows. Rapoport (2000, p. 212), moreover, reports that at the Center his closest contacts included Alex Bavelas and Duncan Luce.

The Center's second year, 1956, attracted both James S. Coleman from Columbia and Leon Festinger, who was then at Stanford but who had been involved in network research at both MIT and Michigan. And in the third year, the fellows included Karl W. Deutsch, who was involved in the second MIT effort, Theodore M. Newcomb from Michigan and Harrison C. White, who was then at Johns Hopkins University but who would later spearhead the second Harvard program. In 1958 Robert P. Abelson from Yale who had been involved in the first MIT thrust, Ronald Lippitt from Michigan and Ithiel de Sola Pool, who was part of the second MIT effort, were at the Center. Although there is no way of knowing who influenced whom among these diverse network scholars, the Center did at least provide the opportunity for a number of individuals who came from different traditions in social network research to meet and exchange ideas.

9.2 Computer Programs

Computers have played a key role in the development of social network analysis. In fact, Alvin W. Wolfe (1978) argued that the field could not have developed without them. The special procedures entailed in the analysis of relation-based data have from the beginning required the development of programs tailored to social network applications.

The earliest of these special purpose programs were all relatively simple and task-specific (Freeman, 1988). In the late 1950s James S. Coleman and Duncan MacRae (1960) produced a computer program that was designed to find groups of closely linked individuals in a social network data set. Later, Coleman's graduate student Seymour Spilerman produced a new algorithm that refined and extended their approach (1966).

Soon thereafter Samuel Leinhardt (1971) attacked a very different kind of problem. He wrote a program, SOCPAC I, to tabulate the various kinds of pairs and triples that can be found in social network data. That same year Gregory Heil and Harrison White introduced BLOCKER, a program designed to uncover actors who occupied similar positions in the overall structure. And in 1972 Richard D. Alba and Myron P. Gutmann (1972) returned to the original problem of uncovering groups. They wrote a program, SOCK, and Alba added another, COMPLT, that took another approach to specifying groups. A year later H. Russell Bernard and Peter D. Killworth (1973) produced still another group-finding program, CATIJ, based on yet another algorithm.

The program CONCOR was introduced in 1975 by Ronald L. Breiger, Scott A. Boorman and Phipps Arabie (1975). It was designed to find not groups, but collections of individuals occupying similar structural positions in a network. The next year, Gregory H. Heil and Harrison C. White (1976) produced a new version of the BLOCKER program that provided another way to find equivalent structural positions. And that same year Ronald S. Burt produced a program called STRUCTURE that took a third approach to the same task.

William D. Richards (1975) developed NEGOPY—another group finder—based on still another algorithm. Stephen B.

Seidman and Brian L. Foster (1978) released SONET, a collection of graph theoretic tools for dealing with kinship relations. In 1979 I wrote a program, CENTER, that used several algorithms to determine the extent to which individuals occupied central positions in their social networks. And in 1981 a group in the Netherlands, including Robert Mokken, Frans Stokman and Jac M. Anthonisse, developed another graph theoretic program, GRADAP. This program, like my program, CENTER, focused particularly on uncovering central positions. And finally, that same year, Peter Carrington and Gregory H. Heil wrote COBLOC, yet another program designed to uncover equivalent structural positions.

These early programs varied widely. They were concerned with groups, positions, centrality, kinship structure and distributions of structural properties. This kind of variation suggests again that the early social network community was, as I have argued, diverse. But at the beginning of the 1980s various attempts were made to tie all of these separate approaches together by producing a general-purpose network analysis program.

Gregory H. Heil, working at the University of Toronto, made an effort to produce an integrated set of network analysis tools. Douglas R. White and Lee D. Sailer at the University of California at Irvine made a similar attempt, as did J. Clyde Mitchell, Clive Payne and David Deans at Oxford University. Unfortunately, none of these efforts panned out; none produced a program for general use.

But in 1983 Franz Urban Pappi and Peter Kappelhoff of Christian-Albrechts-Universität in Kiel produced a general-purpose network analysis program called SONIS (Pappi and Stelck, 1987). And that same year, working with a team at the University of California at Irvine, I produced the first version of a program called UCINET. Since then, UCINET has been refined and extended, first in Version 3.0 through the efforts of a post-doctoral student, Bruce MacEvoy, and more recently in later versions by Stephen P. Borgatti and Martin G. Everett. (My involvement in these later versions has been peripheral.) In any case, both SONIS and UCINET were explicitly designed to include all the procedures that network analysts—regardless of their background—might want to use.

At about the same time, changes were made to both Burt's STRUCTURE and Mokken, Stokman and Anthonisse's GRADAP. In both cases the authors expanded their programs in order to include other procedures. Thus, they both moved in the direction of providing general-purpose programs for social network analysis.

These four programs, then—STRUCTURE, GRADAP and particularly SONIS and UCINET—all made an attempt to include the full range of network analytic procedures. All four have gone through several revisions and all are still being distributed. It seems reasonable to conclude that by providing a standard approach to data analysis, these programs played a role in the development of the social network research community. Peter V. Marsden argued that they did just that:

> *I think the availability of general-purpose, easy-to-use software in the form of UCINET (as early as version 3.0) has made a major difference in our capacity to teach these methods and plausibly urge others to use them. The various discrete packages generated by others have provided useful analyses, but they tended to be specialized to the purposes of their authors, with idiosyncratic data/input requirements; it was hard to make use of multiple methods without doing a lot of cumbersome data transformations and so on. Only with the development of a relatively comprehensive and catholic suite of programs could general-purpose courses be mounted that permitted students to undertake real analyses. You, Steve, and Martin deserve a lot of credit for that, and this program (others like GRADAP could be mentioned as well, though my own view is that other programs have a considerably narrower breadth of application) has to my mind made a signal difference in making social networks accessible to quantitative literates with modest training in mathematics.*

9.3 Conferences

Conferences that brought people from different schools of social network analysis together were also important in building bridges among them. The first step in that direction was taken in 1972 (Mullins and Mullins, 1973, p. 261). In June of 1972 Harrison White organized a conference in Camden, Maine. It included White and his students as well as Steven D. Berkowitz, a graduate student at Brandies University[53], Daniel Bertaux, a French sociologist, Tsuneo Ishikawa, a Harvard economist, and two prominent sociologists from the University of Chicago, Otis and Beverly Duncan. It also included two sociologists from Dartmouth, James A. Davis and Joel Levine. For the most part, then, this was a Harvard "in-house" meeting. But it did involve enough outsiders to begin to build some intellectual bridges.

In the spring of 1974, H. Russell Bernard, an anthropologist at West Virginia University, made a major step toward bringing the separate schools together. He received support from the Mathematical Social Science Board to hold a small meeting at his university. His attempt was to bring together a small collection of mathematicians, anthropologists and sociologists, all active in social network analysis. The participants included a mathematical statistician, Paul Holland; a mathematical physicist, Peter Killworth; four anthropologists, Bernard himself, Manuel Carlos, Douglas R. White and Alvin Wolfe; and four sociologists, Patrick Doreian, Mark Granovetter, Samuel Leinhardt and me. Holland and Leinhardt had been working together as a team, as had Killworth and Bernard.

Each of these participants gave a formal presentation. We spent two days listening to one another. My impression at the time was that each participant had his own more or less idiosyncratic conception of what social network analysis was all about. There turned out to be too few shared understandings to allow for easy communication. Many of us wound up with the impression that the other speakers didn't fully understand what network analysis was all about—they didn't quite "get the pic-

---

[53]Although Berkowitz was not a Harvard student, his wife, Harriet Friedman, was at the time a graduate student there.

ture." However, because this meeting called attention to that problem, it encouraged the participants to try to work out ways to communicate.

In December of that same year Forrest R. Pitts, a University of Hawaii geographer, set up the first of a series of four annual meetings on social networks. The four meetings were sponsored by the Social Sciences and Linguistics Center of the University of Hawaii. At the first meeting, all the participants but Pitts were sociologists and all but two worked at the University of Hawaii.

Those attending the second meeting were mostly the same people who had attended the first. They were still primarily sociologists and most were local University of Hawaii faculty and students. But the third meeting, in 1976, was different. The presence of participants from other places and other disciplines began to give the meeting a more cosmopolitan flavor. That meeting was attended, for example, by two communications scientists, Everett M. Rogers from Stanford and Lawrence Kincaid from the East-West Center in Hawaii.

And Pitts's fourth meeting, in December 1977, was larger and even more interdisciplinary. Those who attended included communications scientists; geographers; psychiatrists; an anthropologist, Brian L. Foster of the State University of New York at Binghamton; a management scientist; and more outside sociologists, including John Sonquist from the University of California, Santa Barbara.

Pitts's aim in organizing these meetings was an attempt to diffuse the social network approach to a wider audience. Over the four year period he did just that, and quite successfully. The first meeting was attended primarily by students and faculty from the University of Hawaii (80%). Moreover, 90% of those present were sociologists. But only 42% of those attending the last meeting were locals and only 53% were sociologists.

In August of 1974 the International Sociological Association held its World Congress in Toronto. Barry Wellman and his wife, Beverly, organized a one-day conference on social network analysis to coincide with the end of those meetings. The Department of Sociology and the Centre for Urban and Community Studies of University of Toronto sponsored the conference. Well-

MSSB Social Networks Symp., Hanover, N.H., Sept. 18-21, 1975

Figure 9.6. Participants in the 1975 Dartmouth Conference

man's aim was to stir up international interest in social network research. And since about seventy-five people attended, the meeting provided a step in that direction. As he (Wellman, 2000) described the outcome of that meeting, "Most of us realized that there was more to social network analysis than the little circle with whom we had gone to graduate school."

The first really major international and interdisciplinary meeting of social network researchers was held at Dartmouth University in the summer of 1975. It was sponsored by the Mathematical Social Science Board and organized by Samuel Leinhardt and H. Russell Bernard. Those who attended are shown in Figure 9.6.

The people in Figure 9.6 are a virtual who's who among American and European sociologists and anthropologists who were involved in the study of social networks before 1975. Those who attended were primarily sociologists, but the meeting also included a number of psychologists, anthropologists and mathematicians. Quite a few came from Europe. And seven were among the founders listed above in Chapters 3 through 7. Dorwin Cartwright and Frank Harary were part of the team at Michigan. J. Clyde Mitchell and John A. Barnes were involved in the work at Manchester. Claude Flament was responsible for the development at the Sorbonne. James A. Davis had been a principal figure at Chicago in the late 1960s. And Harrison White was central to the Harvard effort. This meeting, then was a signal effort to link a number of the distinct schools of social network analysis.

In March of 1978 Barry Wellman and his colleagues at Toronto organized a two-day meeting sponsored by the New College of the University of Toronto. Like Pitts's meetings in Hawaii, most participants were local Toronto faculty and students. Charles Tilly had moved to Toronto in 1965 and stayed long enough to hire Wellman. Wellman had gone on to influence the development of the sociology department in the direction of structural analysis. It included Karen Anderson, Steven Berkowitz, Peter Carrington, June Corman, Barry Crump, Bonnie H. Erickson, Harriet Friedman, Leslie Howard, Nancy Howell and Lorne Tepperman. So a meeting dominated by locals could and did still represent a wide range of structural skills and interests.

In addition, various outsiders were invited. Tilly had left Toronto for Michigan in 1969 but he returned for the meeting. Harrison White was there. Outside sociologists included Patrick Doreian from Pittsburgh, Joseph Galaskiewicz from Minnesota, Samuel Leinhardt from Carnegie Mellon, Joel Levine from Dartmouth and me. Rolf Wigand, a communication scientist from Arizona State, was also there, along with two mathematical statisticians, Stanley Wasserman from Minnesota and Paul Holland, who worked at the Educational Testing Service in New Jersey. This was a much smaller meeting than the one held at Dartmouth, but it did attempt to build some bridges among divergent groups.

Another major meeting was held in January of the following year at the East-West Center in Hawaii. It was organized by D. Lawrence Kincaid and sponsored by the Center. Its explicit aim was to bring a collection of communication scientists together with some social network analysts. Kincaid invited about twenty communication scientists including George Barnett, James Danowski, Richard Farace, Peter Monge, Ronald Rice and Joseph K. Woelfel from the U.S. Included also from the Pacific

Figure 9.7. Participants in the 1979 East-West Center Conference

rim were M. Alwi Dahlan and Parsudi Suparlan from Indonesia, Paul-Thomas De Decker and Nancy Pollack from New Zealand and Sea Baik Lee and Heung-Soo Park from Korea. Kincaid asked me to invite some social network people, so I invited H. Russell Bernard, Ronald S. Burt, Patrick Doreian, Brian L. Foster, Sue Freeman, Maureen T. Hallinan and Stephen B. Seidman from the U.S. and Alden S. Klovdahl from Australia. The attendees are shown in Figure 9.7. The meeting succeeded in building long-term ties that cut across the border between the communication scientists and the broader field of network analysis.

These, so far as I can discover, were the meetings that brought representatives of the several "schools" of social network analysis together. As a participant in several of them, I'm certain that they played an important role in building bridges. For example, I first met Mark Granovetter, Paul Holland and Peter Killworth at Bernard's West Virginia meeting. Moreover, I met John Sonquist and Everett Rogers for the first time at Pitts's Hawaii meeting. I met Steve Berkowitz and Joel Levine at Wellman's 1978 Toronto meeting. And I met George Barnett, Maureen Hallinan, Alden Klovdahl, Peter Monge, Ronald Rice and Joseph Woelfel at Kincaid's Hawaii meeting. These all played an important role in my own integration into the field. And I'm sure that others had similar experiences.

Finally, in 1981, Nan Lin organized a meeting in Albany, New York. Lin's invitations were extended only to sociologists. Invitees included Peter V. Marsden, Mark Granovetter, Edward O. Laumann, Peter Blau, Barry Wellman, Bonnie Erickson, Ronald S. Burt, James S. Coleman, and Charles Kadushin. Most important from the bridging perspective, however, they also included Karen S. Cook who talked about network exchange the-

Figure 9.8. Barry Wellman

ory. Until that meeting the exchange theorists had been talking only to social psychologists, but this presentation led to a long-term connection between exchange theory and social network analysis.

This meeting produced a book (Marsden and Lin, 1982). Moreover, according to Marsden, it was the source of his personal epiphany. As he put it, that meeting "...signaled (to me, anyhow) that this was something broader than the discrete research projects that I'd been associated with up to then...."

9.4 INSNA and Connections

Perhaps the single most important contribution to the integration of the field was made by Barry Wellman (shown in Figure 9.8). While traveling in Europe, Wellman was struck by the fact that people doing similar structural research were simply not in touch with one another. Then too, Wellman had read the Mullins' review of sociology of science (Mullins and Mullins, 1973). There, the Mullinses had suggested that in order to be successful, any developing field must have an "organizational leader." So in the summer of 1977, after canvassing people working in the area, Wellman decided to do some organizing. He founded INSNA, the International Network for Social Network Analysis.

The home base for INSNA was the University of Toronto. Wellman recruited a large—mostly symbolic—advisory board,[54] and he enlisted a bunch of graduate students to carry some of the load. Originally INSNA had no constitution and no bylaws; Wellman and his students simply did whatever was necessary to start it and keep it going. It began with about one hundred and seventy-five members and in two years their efforts raised the membership to about three hundred. Wellman (2000) described the fields of the members of INSNA in the following words:

> *Sociologists were the largest block then as now, comprising about 40% of the total. Five to ten percent each came from anthropology, psychology, communication science, social work and political science, with one or two from community development, computer science, economics, education, geography, gerontology, history, information science, management science, mathematics, psychiatry, public health, and statistics.*

As part of the formation of INSNA, Wellman began publishing a newsletter, *Connections*. "*Connections* was designed to be a means of fostering intellectual and personal connectivity among network analysts" (Wellman, 2000). Wellman (2000) described its contents:

---

[54]The members are listed in Wellman, 2000.

Connections *had lots of small news bits, meeting calendars, information about computer stuff, teaching aids, membership directories, quirky items about networking in the real world, how-to-do-it articles, literature reviews, position statements, and hundreds of abstracts.*

In 1988 Wellman passed the mantle for both INSNA and *Connections* to the Center for Applied Anthropology at the University of South Florida. Alvin W. Wolfe became the manager of INSNA and Susan Greenbaum became the editor of *Connections*. Later the organization and the newsletter were passed on to Katherine Faust and John Skvoretz at the University of South Carolina. From there it went to Stephen P. Borgatti and Candy Jones at Boston College and on to Martin Everett at Greenwich University in England and then to William Richards at Simon Fraser University in Canada. As a consequence of all these transitions, *Connections* became a refereed journal, but it continues also to maintain its original function as a newsletter.

9.5 Social Networks: The Journal

Barry Wellman founded INSNA as a way of facilitating interpersonal connections among people working in social network analysis. At about the same time, I became increasingly concerned with the difficulty of keeping up with the social network literature. It seemed to me that an ever increasing number of network publications were distributed in literally dozens of journals published in ten or twelve fields in six or seven countries. My thought was that the task of keeping up with that kind of scattered literature was more than a full time job.

It seemed to me that a journal focused on the core issues in social network analysis could begin to tie things together. So I wrote up a prospectus for such a journal and sent it off to seven or eight journal publishers. A couple liked the idea, but one in particular drew my attention. Elsevier Sequoia of Lausanne, Switzerland, expressed enough interest to ask me for a list of potential subscribers from whom they could get an evaluation. I sent a list and they mailed it out. The overall response was positive, but there was a significant minority that argued that social network analysis belonged in sociology — in fact, *was* sociology — and should remain there.

In any case, Elsevier Sequoia decided that there was enough support and went ahead with the project. Barry Wellman and I were at the time involved in a computer-based network[55] and were communicating on a daily basis. INSNA had just been formed and I was a member of its Advisory Committee. So when the journal was approved, Wellman and I made an agreement that it would be associated with INSNA. We talked Elsevier Sequoia into selling subscriptions to INSNA members at a greatly reduced rate.

The first issue of *Social Networks* was published in August of 1978. I was editor and J. Clyde Mitchell and Rolf Ziegler were associate editors. In addition, there was also a large Editorial Board. That first issue finally published the classic fugitive piece by Ithiel de Sola Pool and Manfred Kochen that had been written some twenty years earlier (Pool and Kochen, 1978). Included also were articles by Alvin W. Wolfe, Stephen B. Seidman and Brian L. Foster, Lee Douglas Sailer, and Ove Frank.

Social Networks has appeared regularly ever since that first issue. In 1982, with the publication of Volume 4, the publishing was switched from Elsevier Sequoia to North-Holland, the parent company. At the request of the new publisher we dropped the large editorial board and switched from having two associate editors to having a five-member board of associate editors. Then in July of 1998 Ronald L. Breiger joined me as co-editor.

Over the years *Social Networks* has played an important role in bringing the field together. It publishes materials that are widely cited. As early as 1990 it was ranked 17th in influence within the field of sociology. And, as I already mentioned in Chapter 1, Hummon and Carley (1993) reported that its citation patterns display all the properties of "normal" science.

---

[55] To be described in the next section.

9.6 EIES: The Electronic Information Exchange System

At the beginning of this chapter, I reported that some of the members of the emerging social network community were involved in an internet-like computer hookup. In 1977 the National Science Foundation put out a request for proposals to test the effectiveness of a new computer-based communications system. It was hoped that participation in computer-based communication could "enhance the effectiveness of individuals belonging to a scientific community."

Traditionally it had been assumed that physical proximity among the people involved is necessary for development in an emerging field of science (Mullins and Mullins, 1973). When the builders of a new paradigm were concentrated in a single physical location, frequent and regular contacts could occur naturally. But when the people involved were geographically dispersed it would be difficult and costly for them to get together and develop the needed consensuses. Under such conditions, progress in developing the field would either be retarded or eliminated entirely.

The EIES trials, then, were based on the premise that—even with a heterogeneous set of geographically dispersed scientists—significant communication could be developed if the channels are cheap enough, flexible enough and fast enough. So NSF supported the development of a computer system that could perform like the internet now does. It was called the Electronic Information Exchange System (EIES), and it was developed and run at the New Jersey Institute of Technology.

The EIES facility was designed to be an electronic alternative to face-to-face contacts with their requisite costs in time, effort and money. Participants typed messages or comments on terminals located in their homes or offices or other convenient settings. The EIES system allowed a user to send private messages to individuals or groups, or to participate in "computer-managed conferences" in which the ongoing discussion was permanently recorded and accessible to conference group members. Each participant was also provided with a personal notebook "space" in computer memory for material that was being developed and edited. Notebooks could either be kept private or open to co-authors or readers.

Participation in the system was asynchronous and was based on the telephone hookup of computer terminals. When participants phoned into the system, they automatically received all communications that had been directed toward them by other participants since their last session at the terminal. They could compose responses or new communications and enter them into the system. They could then wait for immediate reactions from others, or they could sign off and return later, missing nothing.

I submitted a proposal to NSF suggesting that since social network analysts were interdisciplinary, geographically dispersed and involved in the development of an emerging specialty, social network analysts would provide a good test of the EIES system. I argued that scientists working with social networks were at a critical point in their development as a community. They should, therefore, be an ideal group to study.

NSF funded my proposal. They chose social network analysis as one of four research groups used to explore the impact of the system. Barry Wellman and I picked forty individuals who were active in social network research as participants. They included twenty-four sociologists, seven anthropologists, two information scientists, two mathematicians, two political scientists, two psychologists and one communications scientist. They were geographically dispersed. There were ten from California, six from Pennsylvania, five from New York, two each from Wisconsin, Illinois and Ontario and one each from eleven other states and two other Canadian provinces. And, most important in the present context, the participants represented a wide range of backgrounds in terms of social network analysis. Participants included representatives from the Harvard, Columbia, Michigan, Chicago and Syracuse "schools" of analysis.

We started the computer project with a face-to-face meeting. It was held at Lehigh University in January of 1978. We then proceeded to a two-year computer-based hookup. Some participants loved the conference, but a few hated it and dropped out.

Those of us who continued with the EIES system for the two years of the project learned a great deal about communicating with other social network specialists. We looked much more like a community at the end of the EIES project than we had at the beginning (Freeman and Freeman, 1980; Freeman, 1984b).

9.7 The Sun Belt and the European Meetings

Another major step toward the integration of the social network community was taken when the Sun Belt Meetings were started. All the earlier meetings had been relatively small and for most of them, attendance had been only by invitation. But in 1980 H. Russell Bernard and Alvin W. Wolfe came up with the idea of having regular annual meetings open to all interested parties. Both Bernard and Wolfe worked and lived in Florida and they reasoned that northerners would appreciate a mid-winter meeting in a warm clime. So they proposed that the meetings be held in February in some spot where the weather could be expected to be mild. They negotiated with Barry Wellman and arranged for their proposed "Annual Sunbelt Social Network Conference" be the official INSNA meeting.

Bernard and Wolfe organized the first two Sunbelt Conferences themselves. The first took place in Tampa in February 1981. The second was also held in Tampa in February of 1982, and it included the added attraction of a keynote address by John Barnes. The weather for both was excellent, and those who attended were delighted with their experience—both the intellectual stimulation and the opportunity to bask in the sun.

After the first two, the Sunbelt meetings began to alternate between the east and the west coasts. They tended to attract mostly North Americans, though there were others, particularly some Europeans, who did attend. But because of the added cost in time and money for travel, many European network analysts were unable to cross the ocean. So in 1989, Frans N. Stokman organized the first of a series of European social network conferences patterned after the Sun Belt Conferences. The first was held in June at Stokman's home university, the University of Groningen. Edward O. Laumann gave the keynote speech.

Both conferences continued—the Sun Belt annually and the European biennially—until it was decided in 1994 to merge the

Sunbelt Meeting	European Meeting	Year	Place	Keynote Speaker
I		1981	Tampa, FL	
II		1982	Tampa, FL	John Bames
III		1983	San Diego, CA	James Coleman
IV		1984	Phoenix, AZ	Harrison White
V		1985	Palm Beach, FL	Linton Freeman
VI		1986	Santa Barbara, CA	J. Clyde Mitchell
VII		1987	Clearwater, FL	Everett M. Rogers
VIII		1988	San Diego, CA	Charles Kadushin
IX		1989	Tampa, FL	Frank Harary
	1st	1989	Groningen, Netherlands	Edward Laumann
X		1990	San Diego, CA	Mark Granovetter
XI		1991	Tampa, FL	James Davis
	2nd	1991	Paris, France	Michel Forsé
XII		1992	San Diego, CA	Peter Blau
XIII		1993	Tampa, FL	A. Kimball Romney
	3rd	1993	Munich, Germany	J. Clyde Mitchell
XIV		1994	New Orleans, LA	Barry Wellman
XV	4th	1995	London, England	Patrick Doreian
XVI		1996	Charleston, SC	Bonnie Erickson
XVII		1997	San Diego, CA	H. Russell Bernard & Peter Killworth
XVIII	5th	1998	Sitges, Spain	Rolf Ziegler
XIX		1999	Charleston, SC	Nan Lin
XX		2000	Vancouver, BC	Linton Freeman
XXI	6th	2001	Budapest, Hungary	Martin Everett
XXII		2002	New Orleans, LA	Philippa Pattison
XXIII		2003	Cancun, Mexico	Alvin Wolfe
XXIV	7th	2004	Portorož, Slovenia	Frans Stokman

Figure 9.9. The Sun Belt and European Meetings

two. So the London meeting in 1995 was both the fourth European meeting and the fifteenth Sun Belt. Since then, the pattern has been to hold two meetings in the U.S. and one in Europe, in a three-year cycle. These meetings and their keynote speakers are shown in Figure 9.9.

Along with the computer programs and the journals, these meetings have gone a long way toward knitting the emerging social network community together. Attendance has grown consistently. It is hard to overestimate the importance of these annual meetings in integrating the field.

9.8 The Role of UCI

I have mentioned the University of California, Irvine, at various points in this discussion. The fact is that UCI has contributed to the development of the social network community in several important ways. I will wind up this chapter by discussing some of those contributions.

Perhaps the single most important factor that led to the development of social network analysis at UCI is the flexible structure that James G. March built into the original School of Social Sciences in 1964. March was the founder and first dean of the school.

In addition, March hired John P. Boyd, who had been trained by Anatol Rapoport and the Michigan group in the 1970s. From the beginning Boyd was active in social network research (Boyd, 1969). Then in 1976, the Irvine Program in Comparative Culture hired Douglas R. White. White had been trained by Harary at Michigan and was also interested in social networks. Boyd and White met and arranged to teach a graduate seminar on network analysis in 1977. Lee D. Sailer was one of the students in their seminar and I was one of the visitors who was invited to give presentations there.

Largely through the efforts of White and William Batchelder, I was hired as Dean of the School of Social Sciences and started work there in the summer of 1979. Doug White had already obtained funding in 1978 to start a Focused Research Project in social network analysis at UCI. Its original members included, in addition to White, E. Mansell Pattison from the Department of Psychiatry, James Meehan and Richard Granger from the Department of Computer Science, and Lamar F. Hill from the History Department. In 1979 John Boyd and I joined the project. And, in the next few years, several other School of Social Sciences faculty, A. Kimball Romney, William Batchelder, Michael Burton, R. Duncan Luce and David Smith were added to the project group.

This project brought the faculty who were interested in social networks together on a regular basis. It also permitted the faculty at UCI to develop a regular relationship with the social network group at UC Santa Barbara. At the time, the Santa Barbara group included Dorwin Cartwright, Lawrence Hubert, Noah Friedkin, Eugene Johnsen and John Sonquist among the faculty as well as their student Hugh Kawabata, who had earlier been my undergraduate student at the University of Hawaii. For several years interested parties from both campuses met regularly either at UCI or at UCSB.

The project provided the funds that permitted UCI to host a sponsored social network meeting. A. Kimball Romney, Douglas White and I organized that meeting in Laguna Beach in 1980. Those who attended and presented papers included psychologists, Phipps Arabie and William Batchelder; sociologists, Steven Berkowitz, Phillip Bonacich, Scott A. Boorman, Ronald S. Burt, Patrick D. Doreian, Linton C. Freeman, Gregory Heil, Edward O. Laumann, Peter Marsden and John A Sonquist; anthropologists, John P. Boyd, Brian L. Foster, J. Clyde Mitchell, A. Kimball Romney and Douglas R. White; communication scientists, Ronald Rice and William Richards; and mathematicians, Stephen Seidman and David Strauss. It brought together people from several of the earlier research traditions and served as the final step in knitting the broad social network community together. The papers presented at that meeting were later published as a book (Freeman, White and Romney, 1989).

And finally, the project also facilitated the development of a PhD concentration in social network analysis at UCI. Because its founding dean, James G. March, had designed the School of Social Sciences to be maximally flexible, it was simple to institute a new program within the school. The school faculty who had been associated with the Focused Research Project became the faculty of the new program. And they were joined later by Danching Ruan who joined the UCI faculty in Social Ecology after completing her PhD at Columbia under the guidance of Ronald Burt and Peter Blau.

Very soon the program at UCI began to attract students. The PhDs coming out of the UCI program include a number that are now making contributions to social network analysis: Narda Alcántara Valverde, Ece (Kumbasar) Batchelder, Stephen P. Borgatti, Timothy Brazill, Bret Breslin, Devon Brewer, Silvia Casasola, Malcolm Dow, Katherine Faust, Sue C. Freeman, Rick Grannis, Ti-Lien Hsia, Jeffery Johnson, Alaina (Michaelson) Kanfer, David Krackhardt, Alexandra Maryanski-Turner, Keiko Nakao, Karl Reitz, Lee Sailer, Ryuhei Tsuji, Cynthia Webster and Susan Weller.

In addition, the program at UCI was able to recruit a number of distinguished social network analysts as visiting faculty. These included Ronald Burt, James Coleman, Patrick Doreian, Frank Harary, H.Gilman McCann, David Strauss, Harrison C. White and Alvin Wolfe, all from the United States, William Richards from Canada, Alden Klovdahl from Australia, Narçiso Pizaro from Spain, Vincent Duquenne from France and Wenhong Zhang from the People's Republic of China.

At the same time, the program attracted post-doctoral students including Bruce MacEvoy and John Roberts from the U.S., Martin Everett from Great Britain, Hiroshi Inoye from Japan, Evelien Zeggelink from the Netherlands and Eric Widmer from Switzerland. And in 1995 the eminent German network analyst, Thomas Schweizer, brought ten of his graduate students from the University of Cologne to UCI for a five-week visit. Two of those students, Christine Avenarius and Michael Schnegg, and another German graduate student, Kai Jonas from the University of Göttingen, all maintained residence at UCI for extended periods.

In addition, the Program in Mathematical Behavioral Science at UCI obtained the National Science Foundation support for a second social network meeting. William Batchelder organized that second meeting which was held at UCI in August of 1991. It brought together six mathematicians who had not previously been involved in social network research, Ernest Adams, J. P. Barthelemy, Ian Carlson, Margaret B. Cozzens, Jean-Paul Doignan and Geoffrey Iverson. There were fourteen members of the social network community including five of our own mathematicians: Martin Everett, Eugene Johnsen, Stephen Seidman, Tom A. B. Snijders and Stanley Wasserman. The other network people who attended were Stephen P. Borgatti, John Boyd, Patrick Doreian, Katherine Faust, Alaina Michaelson, Philippa Pattison, A. Kimball Romney, Batchelder himself and me.

All these developments were made possible by the support of the deans of the UCI School of Social Sciences. During my service as dean I consciously tried to build the social network emphasis. Then William Schoenfeld took over as dean in 1982. He was also supportive, particularly for the first several years of his term. In the 1980s and 90s, then, UCI became a prominent center of social network activity. At the same time it took the lead in integrating the several strands of the social network approach.

The 1980s and 90s witnessed the integration of the several "schools" of social network analysis that emerged earlier. Here I have reviewed some of the bases for that integration. Some forces toward integration were probably more or less accidental—like the mobility of individuals among the network centers. But I suspect most of the integration that occurred resulted from conscious attempts by various individuals to bridge the potentially competing "schools." Without a great deal of effort toward developing general-purpose computer programs, organizing face-to-face and computer-mediated conferences, producing core publications and arranging for international meetings, we would not have been able to develop the kind of intellectual and social community that exists today.

Chapter 10

A Summary and Some Surprises

Like any historical account, this one undoubtedly reflects the biases of the reporter. But I hope that my biases and preconceptions have not completely warped the present account. Indeed, in preparing this book, I have continually been surprised. A great deal of the material reported here was new to me, discovered only as I set about writing the history of social network analysis.

Like many earlier writers (Leinhardt, 1977; Marsden and Lin, 1982; Degenne and Forsé, 1994; Wasserman and Faust, 1994), when I began this work I believed that Jacob L. Moreno was *the* major intellectual force behind the emergence of social network analysis. So I was startled by the relatively small number of network analysts who credited J. L. Moreno with providing an important intellectual antecedent for their work.

Perhaps the consensus that Moreno's impact was not that great is justified. In Chapter 2, I described the work of a number of others—particularly those working in educational and developmental psychology. These included Almack, Wellman, Bott and Hagman. These investigators had been the earlier innovators; they had established many of the practices of sociometry before Moreno introduced that perspective in the early 1930s. And in Chapter 3, I suggested that many of the parts of Moreno's work that are most memorable—the systematic parts—were probably all the contributions of Helen Jennings, not of Moreno.

The principal factor in people's refusal to credit Moreno, however, probably results from Moreno's own character. As I suggested in Chapter 3, his inclination toward paranoia tended to drive others away.

Despite all this, I still believe that Moreno was a very major figure in the history of the field. Reading the 1934 edition of *Who Shall Survive*, one can't help but be struck by the creativity and the richness of imagination displayed there. There is practically no idea or practice in contemporary social network analysis that is not present in some form in that book. If we now fail to acknowledge his contributions, along with those of Helen Jennings, we will be diminished thereby.

Another major surprise probably stems from my training as a sociologist. I was struck by the importance of the historical role played by kinship in social network analysis. An anthropologist might have taken that for granted, but sociologists less often think of kinship as belonging to their field. The fact is that by far the earliest example of a systematic network approach was focused on kinship. In the eighth century, drawings of trees were used to depict kinship structures. That was far before any other kinds of explicit network-based practices emerged. Moreover, many other early contributions were concerned with the study of kinship. The mathematical contributions of Macfarlane, and of Bienaymé, Galton and Watson all dealt with kinship. The massive data set collected by Morgan was also focused on kin relations.

For me, another surprise was the sheer number of unheralded innovators who had developed ideas and tools that anticipated current practice in social network analysis. These include, of course, the educational and developmental psychologists mentioned in Chapter 2, but they also include a great many of the contributors discussed in Chapters 4 through 7.

When they deal with work prior to Moreno at all, network analysts generally credit Georg Simmel's contributions. And in treatments of groups, they sometimes cite early sociologists like Tönnies, Durkheim and Cooley (Freeman, 1992; 2002). Hobson has been cited as at least a minor contributor to the study of corporate interlock (Fennema and Schijf, 1978/79), and Galton and Watson have been described as providing an early example of probability-based social network modeling (Mullins and Mullins, 1973).

But nowhere could I find any discussion of the centrality of the structural perspective in the thought of Auguste Comte. Like most American sociologists, I had the works of Durkheim, Marx and Weber drummed into my head in my graduate training. Comte, however, was barely mentioned. So in preparing this book, I was startled to discover that the man who founded sociology was a structural thinker. In preparing this treatment I read a great deal of Comte in the original as well as the wonderful English translation produced by Harriet Martineau. These sources, as I indicated in Chapter 2, contained a clear statement of a surprisingly modern and genuinely structural viewpoint.

The structural ideas of LeBon have similarly been ignored, as has the systematic collection of data by Huber. Huber is known in ethology (Wilson, 1971, p. 299) but has not been recognized by social network analysts. Morgan and Macfarlane, moreover, are unrecognized in the field. And social network analysts have not awarded Bienaymé's probabilistic solution to the problem of the disappearance of family names the recognition it deserves, even though his contribution was correct and was presented long before the work of Galton and Watson,.

But by far the most unexpected discovery to me was the fact that in the early 1930s, while Moreno and Jennings were developing the structural perspective, a parallel development was taking place at Harvard. From my perspective, this finding was particularly unanticipated since the main intellectual force behind it turned out to be W. Lloyd Warner. I had met Warner when I was growing up and lived near the University of Chicago. I always had the impression that he was a relatively minor figure in the Anthropology Department, certainly not of the stature of some of his colleagues, like Fred Eggan and Robert Redfield.

This impression probably resulted from the fact that by the time he got to Chicago, Warner had become a very unorthodox anthropologist. In the first place, he had focused all his post-Australia work on modern Americans rather than studying exotic peoples. And more important, once he arrived in Chicago, he abandoned standard anthropological research altogether. Instead, he joined his former student Burleigh Gardner and conducted small, unpublished studies that attempted to solve problems faced by particular businesses and industries. Certainly this was not considered proper anthropology in that period.

But during his years at Harvard, Warner had been an intellectual fireball. He had been a major figure in both the Anthropology Department and the Business School. And he had influenced his colleagues, like Roethlisberger and Mayo, and his students, like Davis, Gardner, Chapple and Arensberg, to embrace his structural perspective in their research. Warner and his Harvard associates turn out to have produced a very early form of social network analysis. They deserve full credit for that accomplishment.

For the most part, writers who deal with the post-Moreno-pre-White era refer only to the developments by British social anthropologists (Seidman and Foster, 1978; Scott, 1992; Wolfe, 1978). There, the names that are typically introduced include John Barnes, Elizabeth Bott and J. Clyde Mitchell. Sometimes Max Gluckman and Sigfried Nadel are included and, less often, A. R. Radcliffe-Brown is mentioned in that context.

My reading departs from that conventional wisdom. I have suggested here that Radcliffe-Brown was not only *the* key figure in introducing structural ideas into British social anthropology, but that he had huge influences in France and the United States as well. In Britain, R-B's structural thinking was reflected in the works of Firth, Fortes, Evans-Pritchard and Gluckman. And Gluckman went on to conduct the seminar at Manchester that included such notable structural thinkers as Barnes, Bott, Mitchell and Nadel.

In France, Lévi-Strauss acknowledged Radcliffe-Brown's influence on his analysis of kinship. And in America, Radcliffe-Brown's impact was displayed through his influence on the work of his student W. Lloyd Warner. All of Warner's research embodied the structural approach he learned from R-B, and he passed that approach on to his colleagues and students at Harvard.

I had not expected the relatively large impact of the political scientist Karl Deutsch. In the 1950s, I had read some of Deutsch's research that embodied a structural perspective, but I never realized that he had been influential in the development of social network analysis. I did not, therefore, anticipate that his structuralism had a direct influence on such major figures as Anatol Rapoport, Ithiel de Sola Pool, Manfred Kochen and Harrison White. Clearly, Deutsch had a notable impact on the development of the field.

Finally, another revelation for me involved the discovery of the relatively large amount of social network research that was conducted in the period between the decline of sociometry at the end of the 1930s and the explosion at Harvard in the 1970s. The conventional wisdom seems to suggest that this was a period during which network research languished. Yet, as I suggested in earlier chapters, I was able to uncover twelve settings in which research was conducted that embodied all four of the defining features of modern social network analysis. And I am certain that there were others that I simply missed. In any case, it is clear that social network analysis was alive and well in the 40s, 50s and 60s.

After the second Harvard thrust, led by Harrison White in the early 1970s, it became obvious that social network analysis was here to stay. I have argued that modern social network analysis in all of its several forms has been with us since the early 1930s. But it finally emerged as a unified and recognized perspective when those several strands were knit together at the end of the 1970s. Many individuals, including H. Russell Bernard, D. Lawrence Kincaid, Nan Lin, Forrest Pitts and Alvin Wolfe played major roles in bringing them all together. Then too, the EIES computer conference, the journal *Social Networks* and the commitment of the School of Social Sciences at UCI all helped.

But by far the greatest contributor to the unification of the field was Barry Wellman. Wellman held early meetings. Wellman founded the International Network for Social Network Analysis. Wellman founded and edited the newsletter and later journal, *Connections*. Wellman was one of the organizers of the social network community and was centrally involved in EIES, the Electronic Information Exchange System. All in all, it is clear that the field of social network analysis as we know it would not exist without the energy and imagination of Barry Wellman.

According to Mullins and Mullins (1973, pp. 27–33) fields are developed by a process of diffusion. A new perspective emerges at a certain university. Students at that university are trained in that perspective. They complete their training and go on to find jobs at other universities. In turn, they expose a new generation of their own students to the perspective, and in that way the perspective is spread.

But that kind of process does not seem to have been operating in the case of social network analysis. The social network perspective apparently was developed in a number of different disciplines, at a number of different universities located in a number of different countries. Then, through the efforts of Barry Wellman and the others discussed in Chapter 9, all of these research efforts were brought together. People from different fields and different traditions have learned to work together in pursuit of a common goal. As I reported in Chapter 1, Hummon and Carley's (1993) analysis of citation patterns showed that network analysts build on each other's work and that the field, therefore, is systematically accumulating knowledge. Let us hope that we can continue to do just that.

This process of coming together seems still to be continuing. In 1998 a young physicist, Duncan J. Watts, worked with a mathematician, Steven H. Strogatz, and together they published an article on the small world phenomenon in *Nature* (Watts and Strogatz, 1998). At that time, they knew very little about the research tradition described here. They cited Milgram's (1967) paper, but were unaware of the earlier work by Pool and Kochen (1978) or the more than 200 follow-up papers on the subject that have been published by network analysts.[56]

---

[56]It should be noted that none of the physicists has cited the Pool and Kochen paper, even though Kochen had a background in physics and was a PhD mathematician. His paper with Pool contains some rather sophisticated mathematics. Moreover, none cited the follow-up by Harrison White (1970b), who was, himself, a PhD physicist.

In any case, Watts and Strogatz argued the generality of the structural paradigm and they succeeded in interesting other physicists in the structural approach to the study of social phenomena. Following the Watts and Strogatz publication, physicists have published 159 papers on the small world alone. In 1998 Collins and Chow published a follow up. And since then, physics contributors have been immensely productive. Typically, they have access to high-prestige journals, like *Nature, Science, Proceedings of the National Academy of Science, Reviews of Modern Physics* and *Physical Review*. As a consequence, they have attracted a lot of attention in the popular press, and the notion of social networks has become very popular.

To date, however, the integration of these newcomers into the social network research community has been less than total. This is illustrated by the clumping displayed in Figure 8.1. That figure is based on data provided by Eugene Garfield, the founder of the Institute for Scientific Information. Garfield did a citation search on titles containing the phrase "small world" and those that cited that early Milgram article. He found 147 papers that cited the Milgram article and 295 others that used the phrase "small world" in their title.

I took the Garfield data and removed those articles that did not cite any of the others and also were not cited by any of the others. That left 395 in the collection. Because citations to the 1967 Milgram article appeared to be limited to using his words, "small world," I dropped the Milgram article from consideration. My aim was to discover the degree to which there were links between the physicists and the traditional social network analysts that went beyond the mention of Milgram.

So I restricted my analysis to the examination of citations within and between these two collections of writers. It turns out that the two represent distinct citation communities. Both cite others in their own community about 98% of the time. The patterning of citations is shown in Figure 10.1 where the social networkers are coded as white points, the physicists are coded as black points and the outsiders (economists, biologists, etc.) are coded as grey points. From the figure it becomes clear that this phenomenon is, at the moment, being studied by two distinct sets of individuals.

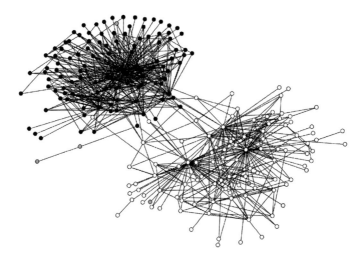

Figure 10.1. Citation patterns in the Small World literature

The consequences of this split are unfortunate. It necessarily leads to wasted effort—reinventing existing tools and rediscovering established empirical results. The physicists Barabasi and Albert (1999), for example, reported a "new" result having to do with the tendency of nodes in a network to display gross inequalities in the numbers of others to which they are linked. And they went on to develop a model designed to explain that tendency. But Paul Lazarsfeld had described the same tendency in 1938 (Moreno and Jennings, 1938), and Derek de Solla Price had developed essentially the same model as early as 1976.

As time passes, however, these physicists show increasing signs that they are being integrated into the social network community. By 1999 Watts had published in the *American Journal of Sociology* and he is now working in the Sociology Department at Columbia University. Moreover, his newer work (e.g. Watts, 2003) displays his increasing awareness of research in the social network tradition. Both Watts and Mark Newman, along with a young German physicist, Bettina Hoser, have attended Sun Belt social network meetings. And both Mark Newman and a Swedish physicist, Petter Holme, have published in the journal, *Social Networks*. So bridges are being built. And if the trends document-

ed in this history hold steady, it will not be long until the physicists who do social network analysis are fully integrated into the
larger social network community.

Finally, there is reason to be hopeful since the field of social
network analysis is currently very "hot," growing at an amazing rate. This is illustrated by Otte and Rousseau's (2002) plot of
the growth in the numbers of network articles abstracted in *Sociological Abstracts* each year from 1974 to 1999. Their plot is reproduced in Figure 10.2. It shows that the study of social
networks is rapidly becoming one of the major areas of social
science research.

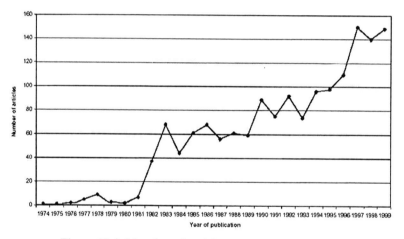

Figure 10.2. Number of social network articles listed in
Sociological Abstracts *by year*

It appears, then, that social network analysis is finally succeeding in providing an alternative to the traditional individu-
alism of most mainstream social research. Network analysis is
booming, and the tendency of social scientists to ignore structure is diminishing. Today, all kinds of social scientists, along
with mathematicians and physicists, have embraced the structural perspective. The study of social structure has come of age.

Acknowledgments

Front Cover. The author's POV-Ray image of data collected by Leo Brajkovich on a small start-up company in California. Points are employees (red points are engineers, blue points are technicians, and yellow points are business people); lines indicate regular communication.

Dedication, p. iv. Photograph of Jacob Moreno taken at the New York Psychodrama Theater in the 1960s. Picture © George S. Zimbel (1965/ 2004 All rights reserved).

Dedication, p. v. Photograph of Harrison White lecturing in the International Graduate Program of Science of Organization, at AILUN (Associazione Istituzione Libera Università Nuorese), Nuoro, Italy. Picture courtesy of Professor Bolacchi, the Chairman and Program Director of the Masters Program at AILUN.

Figure 1.1. Plot adapted by the author from Otte and Rousseau (2002).

Figure 2.1. Image of a stamp issued in 1957 to commemorate the centennial of Comte's death.

Figure 2.2. Photograph by the author.

Figure 2.3. In the public domain.

Figure 2.4. Image from Hobson (1884/1954 in the public domain.

Figure 2.5. Image from Morgan (1851/1997) in the public domain.

Figure 2.6. Image from Macfarlane (1883) in the public domain.

Figure 2.7. Image from Hobson (1884/1954 in the public domain.

Figure 2.8. Courtesy of the Grant Museum of Zoology and Comparative Anatomy, University College, London.

Figure 3.1. Image from Moreno (1934) in the public domain.

Figure 4.1. In the public domain.

Figure 4.2. Image from Warner and Lunt (1941) in the public domain.

Figure 4.3. Image from Roethlisberger and Dickson (1939) in the public domain.

Figure 4.4. Image from Roethlisberger and Dickson (1939) in the public domain.

Figure 4.5. Image of a stamp issued in 1994 as part of the U.S. Postal Service's Black Heritage stamp series.

Figure 4.6. Picture courtesy of Roosevelt University.

Figure 4.7. Image from Davis, Gardner and Gardner (1941) in the public domain.

Figure 4.8. Image from Davis, Gardner and Gardner (1941) in the public domain.

Figure 4.9. Courtesy of the American Sociological Association.

Figure 4.10. Image from Whyte (1943) in the public domain.

Figure 5.1. In the public domain.

Figure 5.2. Courtesy of the MIT Museum.

Figure 5.3. Image from Leavitt (1951) in the public domain.

Figure 5.4. Image drawn by the author.

Figure 5.5. Photograph by Judy Groves © Icon Books Ltd.

Figure 5.6. Image from Lévi-Strauss (1949/1969) in the public domain.

Figure 6.1. Courtesy of Anatol Rapoport.

Figure 6.2. Courtesy of the American Sociological Association.

Figure 6.3. Courtesy of Graham Studios, Philadelphia, PA.

Figure 6.4. Courtesy of the Communications Department, California State University, Fresno.

Figure 6.5. Courtesy of the Royal Anthropological Institute, London.

Figure 6.6. Courtesy of Tim Jake Gluckman.

Figure 6.7. Courtesy of Harvard Square Library.

Figure 6.8. Courtesy of the MIT Museum.

Figure 7.1. Courtesy of the University of Chicago Chronicle.

Figure 9.1. Image of influence data produced by the program, PAJEK, using the Kamada-Kawai spring-embedding routine.

Figures 9.2, 9.3 and 9.4. Images of the EIES data produced by correspondence analysis using the program UCINET.

Figure 9.5. Produced by the author.

Figure 9.6. Courtesy of Samuel Leinhardt.

Figure 9.7. Courtesy of the East-West Center, Honolulu, HI.

Figure 9.8. Courtesy of Barry Wellman.

Figure 9.9. Produced by the author.

Figure 10.1. Data from Eugene Garfield plotted by the author using the spring embedding routine in Borgatti's NetDraw program.

Figure 10.2. Plot adapted by the author from Otte and Rousseau (2002).

References

Abbott, Andrew. 1994. "Review of Identity and Control: A Structural Theory of Social Action." *Social Forces* 73:895–901.

Adams, Stephen B., and Orville R. Butler. 2000. *Manufacturing the Future: A History of Western Electric.* New York: Cambridge University.

Alba, Richard D. 1972. "COMPLT: a program for the analysis of sociometric data and the clustering of similarity matrices." *Behavioral Science* 17:566.

——. 1973. "A graph theoretic definition of a sociometric clique." *Journal of Mathematical Sociology* 3:113–126.

——. 1982. "Taking stock of network analysis: a decade's results." *Research in the Sociology of Organizations* 1:39–74.

Alba, Richard D., and Myron P. Gutmann. 1972. "SOCK: a sociometric analysis system." *Behavioral Science* 17:326.

Allee, Warder Clyde. 1938. *The Social Life of Animals.* New York: W. W. Norton.

Almack, John C. 1922. "The influence of intelligence on the selection of associates." *School and Society* 16:529–530.

Altman, Jeanne. 1974. "Observational study of behavior: Sampling methods." *Behaviour* 49:227–267.

Anderson, Harold H. 1937. "Domination and integration in the social behavior of young children in an experimental play situation." *Genetic Psychology Monographs* 19:343–408.

Anthonisse, Jac M. 1971. "The rush in a directed graph." Amsterdam: Mathematisch Centrum.

Azarian, Reza. 2000. "The Basic Framework in the General Sociology of Harrison C. White." PhD Dissertation in *Sociology*. Stockholm: Stockholm University.

——. 2003. *The General Sociology of Harrison White*. Stockholm: Department of Sociology, Stockholm University.

Baber, Willie. 1999. "St. Claire Drake." Pp. 191–212 in *Pioneers in African American Anthropology*, edited by Ira Harrison and Faye Harrison. Urbana, IL: University of Illinois.

Back, Kurt W. 1951. "Influence through social communication." *Journal of Abnormal and Social Psychology* 46:9–23.

Back, Kurt W., Leon Festinger, Bernard Hymovitch, Harold H. Kelly, Stanley Schachter and John Walter Thibaut. 1950. "The methodology of studying rumor transmission." *Human Relations* 3:307–312.

Ballonoff, Paul A. 1974. "Structural statistics: Models relating demography and social structure with applications to Apache and Hopi." *Social Biology* 20:421–426.

Barabasi, Albert-Laslo, and Reka Albert. 1999. "Emergence of scaling in random networks." *Science* 286:509–512.

Barnes, John A. 1954. "Class and committees in a Norwegian island parish." *Human Relations* 7:39–58.

Barton, Allen. 1968. "Bringing society back in: Survey research and macro-methodology." *American Behavioral Scientist* 12:1–9.

Bateson, Gregory. 2002. *Mind and Nature: A Necessary Unity*. Creskill, NJ: Hampton.

Bavelas, Alex. 1948. "A mathematical model for small group structures." *Human Organization* 7:16–30.

——. 1950. "Communication patterns in task oriented groups." *Journal of the Acoustical Society of America* 22:725–730.

Benedict, Ruth. 1934. *Patterns of culture*. Boston, New York: Houghton Mifflin.

Berge, Claude. 1958. *Théorie des graphes et ses applications*. Paris: Dunod.

Berkowitz, Stephen D. 1982. *An Introduction to Structural Analysis: The Network Approach to Social Research*. Toronto: Butterworths.

Bernard, H. Russell, and Peter D. Killworth. 1973. "On the social structure of an ocean-going research vessel and other important things." *Social Science Research* 2:145–184.

Bernard, H. Russell, Peter D. Killworth, David Kronenfeld and Lee Sailer. 1985. "On the validity of retrospective data: The problem of informant accuracy." in *Annual Reviews in Anthropology*. Palo Alto, CA: Stanford University.

Berry, Brian J. L. 1964. "Cities as systems within systems of cities." *Papers of the Regional Science Association* 13:147–165.

Bhargava, T. N., and Leo Katz. 1963. "A Stochastic-Model for a Binary Dyadic Relation with Applications to Social and Biological Sciences." *Bulletin of the International Statistical Institute* 40:1055–1057.

Bienaymé, Irénée-Jules. 1845. "De la loi de multiplication et de la durée des familles." *Bulletin de la Société Philomathique de Paris* 5:37–39.

Blau, Peter M., and Otis Dudley Duncan. 1967. *The American Occupational Structure*. New York: Wiley.

Blau, Peter M., and Richard A. Schoenherr. 1971. *The Structure of Organizations*. New York: Basic Books.

Boiteux, Yan Demaria. 1958. "Angusto Comte founder of the humanity religion." *Grandes Vultos do Positivismo (em quadrinhos)*. Rio de Janerio: Positivist Church of Brazil.

Boorman, Scott, and Harrison C. White. 1976. "Social structures from multiple networks II: Role structures." *American Journal of Sociology* 81:1384–1446.

Borgatti, Stephen P., Martin G. Everett and Linton C. Freeman. 1999. *Ucinet 5 for Windows: Software for Social Network Analysis*. Natick, MA: Analytic Technologies.

Bott, Elizabeth. 1957. *Family and Social Network*. London: Tavistock Publications.

——. 1971. *Family and Social Network*. New York: Free Press.

Bott, Helen. 1928. "Observation of play activities in a nursery school." *Genetic Psychology Monographs* 4:44–88.

Boyd, John P. 1969. "The algebra of group kinship." *Journal of Mathematical Psychology* 6:139–167.

Braun, Tibor. 2004. "Hungarian Priority in network research." *Science* 18:1744.

Breiger, Ronald, Scott Boorman and Phipps Arabie. 1975. "An algorithm for clustering relational data, with applications to social network analysis and comparison with multidimensional scaling." *Journal of Mathematical Psychology* 12:328–383.

Breiger, Ronald L. 1974. "The duality of persons and groups." *Social Forces* 53:181–190.

Breiger, Ronald L., and Philippa E. Pattison. 1986. "Cumulated social roles: The duality of persons and their algebras." *Social Networks* 8:215–256.

Brown, Lawrence. 1981. *Innovation Diffusion: A New Perspective.* London: Methuen.

Calhoun, Craig. 2003. "Robert K. Merton remembered." in *American Sociological Association, Footnotes.*

Carrington, Peter J., and Greg H. Heil. 1981. "COBLOC: A hierarchical method for blocking network data." *Journal of Mathematical Sociology* 8:103–131.

Cartwright, Dorwin, and Frank Harary. 1956. "Structural balance: A generalization of Heider's theory." *Psychological Review* 63:277–292.

Chapple, Elliot D. 1940. "Measuring human relations: An introduction to the study of interaction of individuals." *Genetic Psychology Monographs.*

——. 1953. "Discussion of patterns in biology, linguistics and culture." Pp. 299–321 in *An Appraisal of Anthropology Today*, edited by Sol Tax, Loren C. Eiseley, Irving Rouse and Carl F. Voeglin. Chicago: University of Chicago.

Châtauneuf, L. F. B. de. 1947. "Mémoire sur la durée des familles nobles de France." *Memoire de l'Académie royale des sciences morale et politiques de l'Institut de France* 5:753–794.

Cocks, Paul. 2001. "Max Gluckman and the critique of segregation in South African anthropology, 1921–1940." *Journal of Southern African Studies* 27:739–756.

Coleman, James S., Elihu Katz and Herbert Menzel. 1957. "The diffusion of an innovation among physicians." *Sociometry* 20:253–270.

Coleman, James S., and Duncan MacRae, Jr. 1960. "Electronic processing of sociometric data for groups up to 1,000 in size." *American Sociological Review* 25:722–727.

Collins, J.J., and Carson C. Chow. 1998. "It's a small world." *Nature* 393: 409–410.

Collins, Randall. 1994. *Four Sociological Traditions*. New York: Oxford University.

Comte, August. 1830–1842. *Cours de philosophie positive* . Paris: J.B. Baillière et fils.

Cooley, Charles Horton. 1909/1962. *Social Organization*. New York: Shocken Books.

Coser, Lewis A. 1977. *Masters of Sociological Thought: Ideas in Historical and Social Context*. New York: Harcourt Brace Jovanovich.

Courrège, Philippe. 1965. "Un modele mathematique des structures elementaires de parente." *L'Homme* 5:248–290.

Dacey, Michael F. 1964. "Two-dimensional random point patterns: A review and an interpretation." *Papers and Proceedings of the Regional Science Association* 13:41–55.

Darwin, Charles. 1859. *On the Origin of Species by Means of Natural Selection, or, The Preservation of Favoured Races in the Struggle for Life*. London: J. Murray.

Davis, Allison, Burleigh B. Gardner and Mary R. Gardner. 1941. *Deep South*. Chicago: University of Chicago.

Davis, James A. 1967. "Clustering and structural balance in graphs." *Human Relations* 20:181–187.

———. 1970. "Clustering and hierarchy in interpersonal relations: testing two graph theoretical models on 742 sociograms." *American Sociological Review* 35:843–852.

Davis, James A., and Samuel Leinhardt. 1971. "The structure of positive interpersonal relations in small groups." in *Sociological Theories in Progress*, edited by Joseph Berger. Boston: Houghton Mifflin.

Degenne, Alain, and Michel Forsé. 1994. *Les Reseaux Sociaux*. Paris: Armand Colin.

Deutsch, Karl W. 1953. *Nationalism and Social Communication: An Inquiry into the Foundations of Nationality*. Cambridge, MA: Massachusetts Institute of Technology.

———. 1963. *The Nerves of Government: Models of Political Communication and Control*. New York: Free Press.

Deutsch, Morton. 1949. "An experimental study of the effects of cooperation and competition upon group process." *Human Relations* 2:199–232.

Doubleday, Thomas. 1842. *The True Law of Population Shewn to be Connected with the Food of the People*. London: Simpkin, Marshall.

Driscoll, Barbara A., Charles Price Loomis, Julian Samora and Gilberto Cardenas. 1993. *La frontera and its people: the early development of border and Mexican American studies*. East Lansing, Mich.: Julian Samora Research Institute, Michigan State University.

Durkheim, Emile. 1893/1964. *The Division of Labor in Society*. New York: Free Press.

Evans-Pritchard, Edward Evan. 1940. *The Nuer: A Description of the Modes of Livelihood and Political Institutions of a Nilotic People*. Oxford: Oxford University.

Fararo, Thomas J. 1963. "Study of Participation Nets." Doctoral dissertation in Sociology. Syracuse, NY: Syracuse University.

——. circa 1964. "Theory of Webs and Social Systems Data." Unpublished note, Syracuse, NY.

Fararo, Thomas J., and Morris H. Sunshine. 1964. *A Study of a Biased Friendship Net*. Syracuse,NY: Syracuse University Youth Development Center.

Faust, Katherine, and John Skvoretz. 2002. "Comparing networks across space and time, size and species." in *Sociological Methodology 2002*, edited by Ross Stolzenberg. Cambridge, MA: Basil Blackwell.

Fennema, Meindert, and Huibert Schijf. 1978/79. "Analysing interlocking directorates: Theory and methods." *Social Networks* 1:297–332.

Festinger, Leon, Stanley Schachter and Kurt W. Back. 1950. *Social Pressure in Informal Groups*. New York: Harper.

Festinger, Leon, and John Walter Thibaut. 1951. "Interpersonal communication in small groups." *Journal of Abnormal and Social Psychology* 46:92–99.

Flament, Claude. 1956. "Influence des changements de réseaux de communication sur les performances des groupes." *Psychologie Française* 1:12–13.

——. 1958*a*. "La performance des groupes de travail, rapports entre la structure de l'activité et celle du réseau de communication." *Année Psychologie* 58:71–89.

——. 1958*b*. "Performance et réseau de communication." *Bulletin du Centre d'Etudes et de Recherches Psychotechniques* 7:97–106.

——. 1961. "Processus d'influence sociale et réseau de communication." *Psychologie Française* 6:115–125.

——. 1963. *Applications of Graph Theory to Group Structure*. Englewood Cliffs, NJ: Prentice-Hall.

Forsyth, Elaine, and Leo Katz. 1946. "A matrix approach to the analysis of sociometric data: Preliminary report." *Sociometry* 9:340–347.

Freeman, Linton C. 1960. "Conflict and congruence in anthroplogical theory." Pp. 93–97 in *Selected Papers of the Vth International Congress of Ethnological and Anthropological Sciences*. Philadelphia: University of Pennsylvania.

——. 1968. *Patterns of Local Community Leadership*. Indianapolis: Bobbs-Merrill.

——. 1984*a*. "Turning a profit from mathematics: the case of social networks." *Journal of Mathematical Sociology* 10:343–360.

——. 1984*b*. "The impact of computer based communication on the social structure of an emerging scientific specialty." *Social Networks* 6:201–221.

——. 1988. "Computer programs in social network analysis." *Connections* 11:26–31.

——. 1989. "Network representations." Pp. 11–40 in *Research Methods in Social Network Analysis*, edited by Linton C. Freeman, Douglas R. White, and A. Kimball Romney. Fairfax, VA: George Mason University.

——. 1992. "The sociological concept of 'group': An empirical test of two models." *American Journal of Sociology* 98:55–79.

——. 2000*a*. "Social network analysis: Definition and history." Pp. 350–351 in *Encyclopedia of Psychology*, edited by A. E. Kazdan. New York: Oxford University.

——. 2000*b*. "Visualizing social networks." *Journal of Social Structure* 1.

——. 2002. "Detectando grupos sociales en datos cuantitativos." in *Análisis de redes, aplicaciones en ciencias sociales*, edited by Jorge Gil Mendieta and Samuel Schmidt. Mexico, DF: Instituto de Investigaciones en Matemáticas Aplicadas y en Sistemas de la Universidad Nacional Autónoma de México.

Freeman, Linton C., Warner Bloomberg, Jr., Stephen Koff, Morris H. Sunshine and Thomas J. Fararo. 1960. *Local Community Leadership*. Syracuse, NY: Syracuse University College.

Freeman, Linton C., Thomas J. Fararo, Warner Jr. Bloomberg and Morris H. Sunshine. 1962. *Metropolitan Decision-Making*. Syracuse, NY: Syracuse University College.

——. 1963. "Locating leaders in local communities." *American Sociological Review* 28:791–798.

Freeman, Linton C., and Sue C. Freeman. 1980. "A semi-visible college: structural effects on a social networks group." Pp. 77–85 in *Electronic Communication: Technology and Impacts*, edited by Madeline M. Henderson and Marcia J. MacNaughton. Boulder, CO: Westview.

Freeman, Linton C., Sue C. Freeman and Alaina G. Michaelson. 1988. "On human social intelligence." *Journal of Social and Biological Structures* 11:415–425.

Freeman, Linton C., Sue C. Freeman and A. Kimball Romney. 1992. "The implications of social structure for dominance hierarchies in red deer (Cervus elaphus L.)." *Animal Behaviour* 44:239–245.

Freeman, Linton C., Douglas Roeder and Robert R. Mulholland. 1980. "Centrality in social networks: ii. experimental results." *Social Networks* 2:119–141.

Freeman, Linton C., A. Kimball Romney and Sue C. Freeman. 1987. "Cognitive structure and informant accuracy." *American Anthropologist* 89:311–325.

Freeman, Linton C., and Barry Wellman. 1995. "A note on the ancestral Toronto home of social network analysis." *Connections* 18:15–19.

Freeman, Linton C., Douglas R. White and A. Kimball Romney. 1989. *Research Methods in Social Network Analysis*. Fairfax, Va.: George Mason University.

French, John R. P. 1950. "Field experiments: Changing group productivity." in *Experiments in Group Productivity*, edited by James Grier Miller. New York: McGraw-Hill.

Galton, Francis. 1908. *Memories of my Life*. London: Methuen.

Galton, Francis, and Henry William Watson. 1875. "On the probable extinction of families." *Journal of the Anthropological Institute of Great Britain and Ireland* 4:138–144.

Garfield, Eugene. 1989. "Manfred Kochen: In memory of an information scientist pioneer qua world brain-ist." *Current Contents* 12:166–169.

Garrison, William L. 1960. "Connectivity of the interstate highway system." *Papers and Proceedings of the Regional Science Association* 6:121–137.

Garrison, William L., Brian J. L. Berry, Duane F. Marble, William B. Nystuen and Richard L. Morrill. 1959. *Studies of Highway Development and Geographic Change*. New York: Greenwood.

George, Sara. 2003. *The Beekeeper's Pupil*. London: Headline Review.

Gillespie, Richard. 1991. *Manufacturing Knowledge: A History of the Hawthorne Experiments*. Cambridge: Cambridge University.

Gluckman, Max. 1955. *Custom and Conflict in Africa*. Oxford: Basil Blackwell.

Goodman, Leo. 1952. "On optimal arrangements in some social learning situations." *Bulletin of Mathematical Biophysics* 14:307–312.

Gould, Peter, and Rodney White. 1974. *Mental Maps*. New York: Penguin.

Guetzkow, Harold, and William R. Dill. 1957. "Factors in the organizational development of task oriented groups." *Sociometry* 20:175–204.

Guetzkow, Harold, and Herbert A. Simon. 1955. "The impact of certain communication nets upon organization and performance in task-oriented groups." *Management Science* 1:233–250.

Gurevitch, Michael. 1961. "The Social Structure of Acquaintanceship Networks." PhD Dissertation in *Economics and Social Science*. Cambridge, MA: Massachusetts Institute of Technology.

Hage, Per, and Frank Harary. 1983. *Structural Models in Anthropology*. Cambridge: Cambridge University.

Hägerstrand, Torsten. 1952. "The Propagation of Innovation Waves." *Lund Studies in Geography, Series B*, volume 4.

Hagman, Elizabeth Pleger. 1933. "The companionships of preschool children." Pp. 10–69 in *University of Iowa Studies in Child Welfare*, edited by George D. Stoddard. Iowa City, IA: University of Iowa.

Harary, Frank. 1953. "On the notion of balance in a signed graph." *Michigan Mathematical Journal* 2:143–146.

———. 1955. "On local balance and N-balance in signed graphs." *Michigan Mathematical Journal* 3:37–41.

Harary, Frank, Robert Zane Norman and Dorwin Cartwright. 1965. *Structural Models: An Introduction to the Theory of Directed Graphs.* New York: Wiley.

Harary, Frank, and Robert Zane Norman. 1953. *Graph Theory as a Mathematical Model in Social Science.* Ann Arbor, MI: University of Michigan.

Harary, Frank, and Ian C. Ross. 1957. "A procedure for clique detection using the group matrix." *Sociometry* 20:205–215.

Hare, A. Paul, and June Rabson Hare. 1996. *J. L. Moreno.* London: Sage.

Heider, Fritz. 1946. "Attitudes and cognitive organization." *Journal of Psychology* 21:107–112.

Heil, Gregory H., and Harrison C. White. 1976. "An algorithm for finding simultaneous homomorphic correspondences between graphs and their image graphs." *Behavioral Science* 21:26–35.

Helmers, Hendrika M., Robert J. Mokken, Roelof C. Plijter and Frans J. Stokman. 1975. *Graven naar Macht. Op zoek naar de kern van de Nederlandse economie (Traces of Power. In Search of the Core of the Dutch Economy).* Amsterdam: Van Gennep.

Hénaff, Marcel. 1998. *Claude Lévi-Strauss and the Making of Structural Anthropology.* Minneapolis: University of Minnesota.

Heyde, Cristopher C., and Eugene Seneta. 1977. *I. J. Bienaymé: Statistical Theory Anticipated.* New York: Springer-Verlag.

Hobson, John A. 1884/1954. *The Evolution of Modern Capitalism; A Study of Machine Production.* London, New York: Allen & Unwin, Macmillan.

Holland, John B., and Charles Price Loomis. 1948. "Goals of life of rural ministers." *Sociometry* 11:217–229.

Homans, George Caspar. 1941. *English Villagers of the Thirteenth Century.* Cambridge, MA: Harvard University.

——. 1950. *The Human Group.* New York: Harcourt, Brace.

——. 1984. *Coming to My Senses: The Autobiography of a Sociologist.* New Brunswick, NJ: Transaction Books.

Homans, George Caspar, and Charles P. Curtis, Jr. 1934. *An Introduction to Pareto: His Sociology.* New York: Alfred A. Knopf.

Huber, François, and Charles Bonnet. 1792. *Nouvelles observations sur les abeilles: adressâees áa M. Charles Bonnet.* Geneve: Barde Manget.

Huber, Pierre. 1802. "Observations on several species of the genus Apis, known by the name of humble bees, and called Bombinatrices by Linneaus." *Transactions of the Linnean Society of London* 6:214–298.

——. 1810. *Recherches sur les moeurs des fourmis indigenes*. Paris: Chez J. J. Paschoud.

Hummon, Norman P., and Kathleen M. Carley. 1993. "Social networks as normal science." *Social Networks* 15:71–106.

Jack, Lois M. 1934. "An experimental study of ascendant behavior in preschool children." *University of Iowa Studies in Child Welfare* 9:9–65.

Jeidels, Otto. 1905. "Das Verhaltnis der deutschen Grossbanken zur Industrie mit besonderer Berucksichtigung der Eisenindustrie: Abschnitt II: Die Entwicklung der Grossbanken." PhD Dissertation. Friedrich-Wilhelms-Universitat zu Berlin.

Jennings, Helen H. 1943. *Leadership and Isolation: A Study of Personality in Interpersonal Relations*. New York: Longmans.

Jerábek, Hynek. 2001. "Paul Lazarsfeld —the founder of modern empirical sociology: a research biography." *International Journal of Public Opinion Research* 13:229–244.

Josselin de Jong, J. P. B. de. 1970. *Levi-Strauss's Theory on Kinship and Marriage*. Leiden: E. J. Brill.

Kamada, Tomihisa, and Satoru Kawai. "An algorithm for drawing general undirected graphs." *Information Processing Letters* 31:7–15.

Katz, Elihu, and Paul F. Lazarsfeld. 1955. *Personal Influence*. New York: Free Press.

Katz, Leo. 1947. "On the matric analysis of sociometric data." *Sociometry* 10:233–241.

Katz, Leo, and J. H. Powell. 1955. "Measurement of the tendency toward reciprocation of choice." *Sociometry* 18:659–665.

Kelley, Harold H. 1950. "The warm-cold variable in first impressions of persons." *Journal of Personality* 2:431–439.

Kemeny, John G., J. Laurie Snell and Gerald Luther Thompson. 1957. *Introduction to Finite Mathematics*. Englewood Cliffs, N.J.: Prentice-Hall.

Kendall, David G. 1975. "The genealogy of genealogy branching processes before (and after) 1873." *Bulletin of the London Mathematical Society* 7:225–253.

Klapisch-Zuber, Christiane. 2000. *L'Ombre des Ancêtres: Essai sur l'Imaginaire Médiéval de la Parenté*. Paris: Fayard.

Knoke, David, and James H. Kuklinski. 1982. *Network Analysis*. Beverly Hills, Calif.: Sage.

Kochen, Manfred. 1986. "Candidate's mission statement for American Society for Information Science president, Ballot."

Kuhn, Thomas S. 1962. *The Structure of Scientific Revolutions*. Chicago,: University of Chicago.

Landahl, Herbert D. 1953a. "An approximation method for the solution of diffusion and related problems." *Bulletin of Mathematical Biophysics* 15:49–61.

——. 1953b. "On the spread of information with time and distance." *Bulletin of Mathematical Biophysics* 15:367–381.

Landau, Hyman G. 1951a. "On dominance relations and the structure of animal societies: I. Effect of inherent characteristics." *Bulletin of Mathematical Biophysics* 13:1–19.

——. 1951b. "On dominance relations and the structure of animal societies: II. Some effects of possible social factors." *Bulletin of Mathematical Biophysics* 13:245–262.

——. 1952. "On some problems of random nets." *Bulletin of Mathematical Biophysics* 14:203–212.

——. 1953. "On dominance relations and the structure of animal societies: III. The condition for a score structure." *Bulletin of Mathematical Biophysics* 15:143–148.

Landau, Hyman G., and Anatol Rapoport. 1953. "Contributions to the mathematical theory of contagion and spread of information through a thoroughly mixed population." *Bulletin of Mathematical Biophysics* 15:173–183.

Laumann, Edward O. 1973. *Bonds of Pluralism: The Form and Substance of Urban Social Networks*. New York: Wiley.

Laumann, Edward O., John H. Gagnon, Robert T. Michael and Stuart Michaels. 1994. *The Social Organization of Sexuality*. Chicago: University of Chicago.

Laumann, Edward O., and Louis Guttman. 1966. "The relative associational contiguity of occupations in an urban setting." *American Sociological Review* 31:169–178.

Laumann, Edward O., and David Knoke. 1987. *The Organizational State: Social Choice in National Policy Domains.* Madison, WI: University of Wisconsin.

Laumann, Edward O., and Frans U. Pappi. 1973. "New directions in the study of elites." *American Sociological Review* 38:212–230.

——. 1976. *Networks of Collective Action.* New York: Academic.

Lazarsfeld, Paul F. 1975. "Working with Merton." Pp. 35–66 in *The Idea of Social Structure: Papers in Honor of Robert K. Merton,* edited by Lewis A. Coser. New York: Harcourt Brace Jovanovich.

Lazarsfeld, Paul F., Bernard Berelson and Hazel Gaudet. 1944. *The People's Choice.* New York: Duell, Sloan and Pearce.

Lazarsfeld, Paul F., and Robert K. Merton. 1954. "Friendship as a social process: a substantive and methodological analysis." Pp. 18–66 in *Freedom and Control in Modern Society,* edited by Morroe Berger, Theodore Abel and Charles H. Page. New York: Van Nostrand.

Leavitt, Harold J. 1951. "Some effects of communication patterns on group performance." *Journal of Abnormal and Social Psychology* 46:38–50.

LeBon, Gustave. 1897/1995. *The Crowd.* New Brunswick, N.J.: Transaction Pub.

Leinhardt, Samuel. 1971. "SOCPAC I: A Fortran IV program for structural analysis of sociometric data." *Behavioral Science* 16:515–516.

——. 1977. *Social Networks: A Developing Paradigm.* New York: Academic.

Lettvin, Jerome Y. n.d. "Pitts, Walter." MIT-Encyclopedia of Cognitive Science on the World Wide Web.

Levine, Joel H. 1972. "The sphere of influence." *American Sociological Review* 37:14–27.

Levine, Joel H., and Kathleen M. Carley. 1997. "On with the revolution." Program for *The White Tie Event.* San Diego, CA.

Lévi-Strauss, Claude. 1949/1969. *The Elementary Structures of Kinship.* Boston: Beacon.

——. 1960. "On manipulated sociological models." *Bijdragen tot de Taal-Land- en Volkenkunde* 16:45–54.

Lewin, Kurt. 1936. *Principles of Topological Psychology.* New York: McGraw-Hill.

Lewin, Kurt, Ronald Lippet and Ralph K. White. 1939. "Patterns of aggressive behavior in experimentally created social climates." *Journal of Social Psychology* 10:271–299.

Lewin, Kurt, and Ronald Lippitt. 1938. "An experimental approach to the study of autocracy and democracy: a preliminary note." *Sociometry* 1:292–300.

Lippitt, Ronald, and John R. P. French. 1948. "Research and training: The research program on training and group life at Bethel." *The Group* 2:11–15.

Lippitt, Ronald, and Marian Radke. 1946. "New trends in the investigation of prejudice." *The Annals of the American Academy of Political and Social Science* 244:167–176.

Loomis, Charles P. 1946. "Political and Occupational Cleavages in a Hanoverian Village, Germany: A Sociometric Study." *Sociometry* 9:316–333.

Loomis, Charles P., and Dwight M. Davidson, Jr. 1939. "Sociometrics and the study of new rural communities." *Sociometry* 2:56–76.

Loomis, Charles P., and Reed M. Powell. 1949. "Sociometric analysis of class status in rural Costa Rica—a peasant community compared with an hacienda community." *Sociometry* 12:144–157.

Loomis, Charles P., and Charles Proctor. 1950. "The relationship between choice status and economic status in social systems." *Sociometry* 13:307–313.

Lorrain, Francois P., and Harrison C. White. 1971. "Structural equivalence of individuals in social networks." *Journal of Mathematical Sociology* 1:49–80.

Luce, R. Duncan. 1978. "R. Duncan Luce." Pp. 245–289 in *The Psychologists*, edited by T. S. Krawiek. Brandon, VT: Clinical Psychology Publishing Company.

Luce, R. Duncan, and Albert Perry. 1949. "A method of matrix analysis of group structure." *Psychometrika* 14:95–116.

Lynd, Robert Staughton, and Helen Merrell Lynd. 1929. *Middletown: A Study in Contemporary American Culture.* New York: Harcourt, Brace.

Macfarlane, Alexander. 1883. "Analysis of relationships of consanguinity and affinity." *Journal of the Royal Anthropological Institute of Great Britain and Ireland* 12:46–63.

MacLean, Alair, and Andy Olds. 2001. "Interview with Harrison White."

Maine, Henry. 1861/1931. *Ancient Law*. London: Oxford University.

Malinowski, Bronislaw. 1922. *Argonauts of the Western Pacific; An Account of Native Enterprise and Adventure in the Archipelagoes of Melanesian New Guinea*. London: Routledge and Kegan Paul.

Marineau, René. 1989. *Jacob Levy Moreno, 1889–1974: Father of Psychodrama, Sociometry, and Group Psychotherapy*. London; New York: Tavistock/Routledge.

Marsden, Peter V., and Nan Lin. 1982. *Social Structure and Network Analysis*. Beverly Hills: Sage.

Martineau, Harriet. 1835/2000. *The Positive Philosophy of Auguste Comte*. Kitchner, Ontario: Batoche.

Mayo, Elton. 1933. *The Human Problems of an Industrial Civilization*. New York: Macmillan.

McCann, H. Gilman. 1978. *Chemistry Transformed: The Paradigmatic Shift from Phlogiston to Oxygen*. Norwood, NJ: Ablex.

McPherson, J. Miller, and James R. Ranger-Moore. 1991. "Evolution on a dancing landscape: Organizations and networks in dynamic Blau space." *Social Forces* 70:19–42.

Menzel, Herbert, and Elihu Katz. 1956. "Social relations and innovation in the medical profession." *Public Opinion Quarterly* 9:337–353.

Merton, Robert K. 1998. "Working with Lazarsfeld: Notes and Contexts." in *Paul Lazarsfeld (1901–1976) La sociologie de Vienne – New York*, edited by Jacques Lautman and Bernard-Pierre Lécuyer. Paris: Editions L'Harmattan.

Michaelson, Alaina G. 1990. "Network mechanisms underlying diffusion processes: Interaction and friendship in a scientific community." in *Social Science*. Irvine, CA: University of California.

Mickenberg, Risa, and Joanne Dugan. 1996. *Taxi Driver Wisdom*. San Francisco: Chronicle.

Milgram, Stanley. 1967. "The small world problem." *Psychology Today* 22:61–67.

Mitchell, J. Clyde. 1969. *Social Networks in Urban Situations: Analyses of Personal Relationships in Central African Towns*. Manchester: Published for the Institute for Social Research University of Zambia by Manchester University.

Mokken, Robert J. 1979. "Cliques, clubs and clans." *Quantity and Quality* 13:161–173.

Moreno, Jacob L. 1932. *Application of the Group Method to Classification.* New York: National Committee on Prisons and Prison Labor.

——. 1934. *Who Shall Survive?* Washington, DC: Nervous and Mental Disease Publishing Company.

——. 1937. "Sociometry in relation to other social sciences." *Sociometry* 1:206–219.

——. 1946. *Psychodrama.* Beacon, NY: Beacon.

——. 1953. *Who Shall Survive?* Beacon, N.Y.: Beacon.

——. 1985. *The Autobiography of J. L. Moreno, M. D.* Boston: Harvard Archives.

Moreno, Jacob L., and Helen H. Jennings. 1938. "Statistics of social configurations." *Sociometry* 1:342–374.

Moreno, Jacob L., Helen H. Jennings, Joan H. Criswell, Leo Katz, Robert R. Blake, Jane S. Mouton, Merl E. Bonney, Mary L. Northway, Charles P. Loomis, Charles H. Proctor, Renato Tagiuri and Jiri Nehnevajsa. 1960. *The Sociometry Reader.* Glencoe, IL: Free Press.

Morgan, Lewis Henry. 1851. *League of the Ho-dé-no-sau-nee or Iroquois.* Rochester, NY: Sage.

——. 1851/1997. *Systems of Consanguinity and Affinity of the Human Family.* Lincoln, NE: University of Nebraska.

Morrow, Alfred J. 1947. "In memorandum, Kurt Lewin, 1890–1947." *Sociometry* 10:211–212.

Mullins, Nicholas C., and Carolyn J. Mullins. 1973. *Theories and Theory Groups in Contemporary American Sociology.* New York: Harper & Row.

Nadel, Sigfried F. 1957. *The Theory of Social Structure.* London: Cohen and West.

Nehnevajsa, Jiri. 1956. "Sociometry: Decades of growth." Pp. 48–95 in *Sociometry and the Science of Man*, edited by Jacob L. Moreno. New York: Beacon.

Newcomb, Theodore M. 1961. *The Acquaintance Process.* New York: Holt, Rhinehart, and Winston.

Nordlie, Peter G. 1958. "A longitudinal study of interpersonal attraction in a natural group setting." PhD Dissertation in *Psychology*. Ann Arbor: University of Michigan.

Ore, Øystein. 1963. *Graphs and their uses*. New York: Random House.

Otte, Evelien, and Ronald Rousseau. 2002. "Social network analysis: A powerful strategy, also for the information sciences." *Journal of Information Science* 28:441–453.

Page, Marjorie L. 1936. "The modification of ascendant behavior in preschool children." *University of Iowa Studies in Child Welfare* 12:7–69.

Pappi, Franz Urban, and Klaus Stelck. 1987. "Ein Databanksystem zur Netzwerkanalyse." Pp. 253–265 in *Methoden Netzwerkanalyse*, edited by Franz Urban Pappi. München: Oldenberg.

Pareto, Vilfredo. 1916/1963. *The Mind and Society: A Treatise on General Sociology*. New York: Dover.

Patnoe, Shelley. 1988. *A Narrative History of Experimental Social Psychology: The Lewin Tradition*. New York: Springer-Verlag.

Pearson, Karl. 1914, 1924, 1930. *The Life, Letters and Labours of Francis Galton* (three volumes). London: Cambridge University.

Pepitone, Albert. 1950. "Motivational effects in social perception." *Human Relations* 3:319–348.

Pitts, Forrest R. 1965. "A graph theoretic approach to historical geography." *The Professional Geographer* 17:15–20.

——. 1979. "The medieval river trade network of Russia revisited." *Social Networks* 1:285–292.

Pool, Ithiel de Sola. 1977. *The Social Impact of the Telephone*. Cambridge, MA: Massachusetts Institute of Technology.

——. 1983. "Four unnatural institutions and the road ahead." Pp. 227–237 in *Politics in Wired Nations: Selected Writings of Ithiel de Sola Pool*, edited by Lloyd S. Etheredge. New Brunswick, NJ: Transaction.

Pool, Ithiel de Sola, and Manfred Kochen. 1978. "Contacts and influence." *Social Networks* 1:5–51.

Price, Derek de Solla. 1976. "A general theory of bibliometric and other cumulative advantage processes." *Journal of the American Society for Information Science* 27:292–306.

Radcliffe-Brown, Alfred Reginald. 1940. "On social structure." *Journal of the Royal Anthropological Institute of Great Britain and Ireland* 70:1–12.

——. 1950. *African Systems of Kinship and Marriage.* Oxford: Oxford University.

——. 1952. *Structure and Function in Primitive Society: Essays and Addresses.* Glencoe, IL: Free Press.

——. 1957. *A Natural Science of Society.* Chicago: University of Chicago.

Radcliffe-Brown, Alfred Reginald, and Cyril Daryll Forde. 1950. *African systems of kinship and marriage.* London, New York,: Published for the International African Institute by the Oxford University.

Rapoport, Anatol. 1949*a*. "Outline of a probabilistic approach to animal sociology." *Bulletin of Mathematical Biophysics* 11:183–196.

——. 1949*b*. "Outline of a probabilistic approach to animal sociology II." *Bulletin of Mathematical Biophysics* 11:273–281.

——. 1953. "Spread of information through a population with socio-structrual bias: I. Assumption of transitivity." *Bulletin of Mathematical Biophysics* 15:523–533.

——. 1954. "Spread of information through a population with socio-structural bias. III. Suggested experimental procedures." *Bulletin of Mathematical Biophysics* 16:75–81.

——. 1957. "A contribution to the theory of random and biased nets." *Bulletin of Mathematical Biophysics* 19:257–271.

——. 2000. *Certainties and Doubts.* Montreal: Black Rose Books.

Rapoport, Anatol, and William J. Horvath. 1961. "A study of a large sociogram." *Behavioral Science* 6:279–291.

Rapoport, Anatol, and Lionel I. Rebhun. 1952. "On the mathematical theory of rumor spread." *Bulletin of Mathematical Biophysics* 14:375–383.

Rashevsky, Nicholas. 1949. "Mathematical biology of social behavior." *Bulletin of Mathematical Biophysics* 11:105–111.

——. 1951*a*. "A note on the theory of communication through social channels." *Bulletin of Mathematical Biophysics* 13:139–146.

——. 1951*b*. "A note on imitative behavior and information." *Bulletin of Mathematical Biophysics* 13:147–151.

——. 1968. *Looking at History through Mathematics*. Cambridge, MA: Massachusetts Institute of Technology.

Renshaw, Peter D. 1981. "The roots of peer interaction research." Pp. 1–25 in *The Development of Children's Friendships*, edited by Steven R. Asher and John M. Gottman. Cambridge: Cambridge University.

Richards, William. 1975. *A Manual for Network Analysis (using NEGOPY Network Analysis Program)*. Stanford: Stanford University. .

Roethlisberger, Fritz J. 1977. *The Elusive Phenomena*. Boston, MA: Division of Research, Graduate School of Business Administration, Harvard University.

Roethlisberger, Fritz J., and W. J. Dickson. 1939. *Management and the Worker*. Cambridge, MA: Harvard University.

Rogers, Everett M. 1962. *Diffusion of Innovations*. New York: Free Press.

Rogers, Everett M., and George M. Beal. 1958. "The importance of personal influence in the adoption of technological changes." *Social Forces* 36:328–335.

Rogers, Everett M., and D. Lawrence Kincaid. 1981. *Communication Networks. Toward a New Paradigm for Research*. New York: Free Press.

Rosenthal, Howard. 1960. "Acquaintances and Contacts of Franklin Roosevelt." Bachelor's Thesis in *Political Science*. Cambridge, MA: Massachusetts Institute of Technology.

Sailer, Lee Douglas. 1978. "Structural equivalence: meaning and definition, computation and application." *Social Networks* 1:73–90.

Saussure, Ferdinand de, Charles Bally, Albert Sechehaye and Albert Reidlinger. 1916. *Cours de linguistique générale*. Paris: Payot.

Schachter, Stanley. 1951. "Deviation, rejection and communication." *Journal of Abnormal and Social Psychology* 46:190–208.

Scott, John. 1992. *Social Network Analysis*. Newbury Park, CA: Sage.

——. 2000. *Social Network Analysis*. Newbury Park, CA: Sage.

Seidman, Stephen B., and Brian L. Foster. 1978. "A note on the potential for genuine cross-fertilization between anthropology and mathematics." *Social Networks* 1:65–72.

——. 1979. "SONET-1." *Social Networks* 2:85–90.

Simmel, Georg. 1908/1971. *On Individuality and Social Forms*. Chicago: University of Chicago.

Smith, Sidney L. 1950. "Communication pattern and adaptability of task-oriented groups: An experimental study." Cambridge, MA: Group Networks Laboratory, Research Laboratory of Electronics, Massachusetts Institute of Technology.

Solomonoff, Ray J., and Anatol Rapoport. 1951. "Connectivity of random nets." *Bulletin of Mathematical Biophysics* 13:107–117.

Spencer, Herbert. 1897. *The Principles of Sociology*. New York: Appleton-Century-Crofts.

Spilerman, Seymour. 1966. "Structural analysis and the generation of sociograms." *Behavioral Science* 11:312–318.

Standley, Arline Reilein. 1981. *Auguste Comte*. Boston: Twayne Publishers.

Stokman, Frans N. 1977. "Third World Group Formation in the United Nations. A Methodological Analysis." in *Social Sciences*. Amsterdam: University of Amsterdam.

Stokman, Frans N., Rolf Ziegler and John Scott. 1985. *Networks of Corporate Power: A Comparative Analysis of Ten Countries*. Oxford: B. Blackwell.

Thibaut, John Walter. 1950. "An experimental study of the cohesiveness of underprivileged groups." *Human Relations* 3:251–278.

Tilly, Charles. 1989. "George Caspar Homans and the rest of us: Remarks by Charles Tilly." in *Sociology Lives* (Harvard University Sociology Department Newsletter).

Tobler, Waldo R. 1963. "Geographic area and map projections." *The Geographical Review* 53:59–78.

——. 1965. "Computation of the correspondence of geographical patterns." *Papers and Proceedings of the Regional Science Association* 15:131–139.

Tönnies, Ferdinand. 1855/1936. *Gemeinschaft und Gesellschaft*. East Lansing, MI: Michigan State University.

Tooker, Elizabeth. 1997. "Introduction." in *Systems of Consanguinity and Affinity of the Human Family*. Lincoln, NE: University of Nebraska.

Travers, Jeffrey, and Stanley Milgram. 1969. "An experimental study of the small world problem." *Sociometry* 32:425–443.

Warner, Mildred Hall. 1988. *W. Lloyd Warner: Social Anthropologist*. New York: Publishing Center for Cultural Resources.

Warner, W. Lloyd. 1937. *A Black Civilization*. New York London: Harper & Brothers.

Warner, W. Lloyd, and Paul S. Lunt. 1941. *The Social Life of a Modern Community*. New Haven, CT: Yale University.

Wasserman, Stanley, and Katherine Faust. 1994. *Social Network Analysis: Methods and Applications*. Cambridge: Cambridge University.

Watts, Duncan J. 1999. *Small Worlds: The Dynamics of Networks Between Order and Randomness*. Princeton: Princeton University.

———. 2003. *Six Degrees: The Science of a Connected Age*. New York: W. W. Norton.

Watts, Duncan J., and Steven H. Strogatz. 1998. "Collective dynamics of "small world" networks." *Nature* 393:440–442.

Wech, Barbara A. 1996. "The Lewin/Moreno controversy." *Southern Management Association Proceedings*. 4:21–423.

Wellman, Beth. 1926. "The school child's choice of companions." *Journal of Educational Research* 14:126–132.

Wellman, Barry. 2000. "Networking network analysts: How INSNA (the International Network for Social Network Analysis) came to be." *Connections* 23:20–31.

White, Douglas R., and Karl P. Reitz. 1983. "Graph and semigroup homomorphisms on networks of relations." *Social Networks* 5:193–234.

White, Harrison C. 1963. *An Anatomy of Kinship*. Englewood Cliffs, NJ: Prentice-Hall.

———. 1970a. *Chains of Opportunity; System Models of Mobility in Organizations*. Cambridge, Mass.: Harvard University.

———. 1970b. "Search parameters for the small world problem." *Social Forces* 49:259–264.

White, Harrison C., Scott A. Boorman and Ronald L. Breiger. 1976. "Social structure from multiple networks I: Blockmodels of roles and positions." *American Journal of Sociology* 81:730–781.

Whitehead, Alfred North. 1925. *Science and the Modern World*. New York: Macmillan.

Whyte, William Foote. 1943. *Street Corner Society; the Social Structure of an Italian Slum*. Chicago, IL: University of Chicago.

——. 1994. *Participant Observer: An Autobiography*. Ithaca, NY: ILR.

Wiese, Leopold von, and Hermann Mueller. 1931/1941. *Sociology*. New York: O. Piest.

Wilson, Edward O. 1971. *The Insect Societies*. Cambridge, MA: Belknam.

Winship, Christopher. 1977. "A distance model for sociometric structure." *Journal of Mathematical Sociology* 5:21–39.

Winship, Christopher, and Michael Mandell. 1983. "Roles and positions: A critique and extension of the blockmodeling approach." Pp. 314–344 in *Sociological Methodology, 1983–84*. San Francisco: Jossey-Bass.

Wolfe, Alvin W. 1978. "The rise of network thinking in anthropology." *Social Networks* 1:53–64.

Yan, Xiaoyan. 1988. "On fuzzy cliques in fuzzy networks." *Journal of Mathematical Sociology* 13:359–389.

Index

Carlos, Manuel, 142
Carlson, Ian, 157
Carnap, Rudolph, 86
Carnegie Mellon University, 88,
  122, 138, 145
Carrington, Peter J., 140, 145
Cartan, Henri, 80
Cartwright, Dorwin, xi, 4, 67, 68,
  71–75, 113, 116, 118, 145, 156
Casasola, Silvia, 157
Chapin, F. Stuart, 36
Chapple, Elliot D., 21, 43, 45, 57–
  58, 60–63, 74, 114, 162
Chase, Ivan, 127
Châtauneuf, L. F. B. de, 28
Chow, Carson C., 165
Christian-Albrechts-University,
  140
Christie, Lee S., 70
Cocks, Paul, 103
Coleman, James S., xii, 96, 97, 98,
  114, 119, 123, 130, 135, 138–
  139, 147, 154, 157
Collins, J. J., 165
Collins, Randall, 43
Cologne, University of, 157
Columbia University, 1, 19, 35,
  38, 40, 62, 70, 90, 92, 94–99,
  108, 115–116, 119, 138, 152,
  156, 166
Colyer, Arthur, 121
Compton, Karl Taylor, 68
computers, 3–4, 126, 132–134,
  136, 139–141, 149–152, 158
computer programs, 6–7, 68, 85,
  95, 96, 99, 114, 116–117, 130,
  132, 136, 138–141, 155–158
Comte, August, 11, 12, 13, 14, 16,
  161
conferences, 117, 142–144, 146,
  151–153, 163
Cook, Karen S., 147

Cooley, Charles Horton, 14, 30,
  160
Copobianco, Michael, 135
Corman, June, 145
Cornell University, 62, 66
Coser, Lewis A., 11, 12
Cottrell, Leonard, 36
Courrège, Philippe, 81
Cozzens, Margaret B., 157
Crump, Barry, 145
Curtis, Charles P., 55
Dacey, Michael F., 84
Dahlan, M. Alwi, 146
Danowski, James, 100, 145
Dartmouth University, 142, 144,
  145
Darwin, Charles, 17, 26
Davidson, Dwight M., 76
Davis, Allison, 43, 45, 51, 53, 55,
  58, 61, 63, 101, 110, 112, 162
Davis, Elizabeth, 43, 45, 51
Davis, James A., xi, 115–116, 119,
  128, 142, 145, 154
Davis, Kingsley, 55
DeDecker, Paul-Thomas, 146
Degenne, Alain, xi, 7, 159
demography, 28, 76, 83
Deutsch, Karl W., 106–109, 119,
  122, 130, 138, 163
Deutsch, Morton, 67–68
Deutsch, Ruth, 106
DeVoto, Bernard, 55
Dickson, William J., 48, 49, 58
Dill, William R., 70
Dodd, Stuart C., 36
Doignan, Jean-Paul, 157
Dominguez, Jorge I., 106
Doreian, Patrick, xi, 135, 142,
  145, 146, 154, 156–158
Doubleday, Thomas, 28
Douglas, Paul, 109
Dow, Malcom, 157

University of Wisconsin, 109
Verba, Sidney, 106
Warner, Mildred Hall, 45, 48, 60
Warner, W. Lloyd, 8, 43–46, 48–
49, 51, 53, 55, 57, 60–63, 74, 76,
81, 101, 114, 128, 161–162
Wasserman, Stanley, 7, 135, 145,
157, 159
Watson, Henry William, 27, 28,
29, 30, 108, 135, 160, 161
Watts, Duncan J., 135, 164, 165,
166
Weber, Max, 161
Webster, Cynthia, xii, 157
Wech, Barbara A., 73
Weil, André, 79–81, 118, 123, 128,
135
Weil, Simone, 78, 80
Weller, Susan, 157
Wellman, Barry, xi, xii, 20, 21,
127, 143–150, 152–154, 159,
163–164
Wellman, Beth, 20, 159
Wellman, Beverly, 143
Wertheimer, Max, 66
Wheeldon, Pru, 4
Wheeler, William, 54
White, Douglas R., xi, xii, 37, 140,
142, 155–156
White, Harrison C., xi, 7–8, 37,
75, 81, 107, 114, 116, 120, 121–
128, 135–136, 138–139, 142,
145, 157, 163, 164
White, Ralph K., 73
White, Rodney, 84
White, William Allison, 36
Whitehead, Alfred North, 2, 48,
54
Whitehead, T. North, 43, 48, 49,
53, 55
Whyte, William Foote, 43, 58–62,
74, 101
Widmer, Eric, 157

Wiese, Leopold von, 16, 30
Wigand, Rolf, 145
Williams, Robin, xii
Wilson, Edward O., 161
Winch, Robert F., 130
Winship, Christopher, 37, 127,
135
Woelfel, Joseph K., 145, 146
Wolfe, Alvin W., xi, 7, 135, 139,
142, 149, 150, 153, 154, 157,
162, 163
Wright, Harold, 48
Yan, Xiaoyan, 37
Zander, Alvin, 41, 67
Zeggelink, Evelien, 157
Zhang, Wenhong, 157
Ziegler, Rolf, xi, 19, 150, 154
Zinzer, Hans, 55